project
RISK
MANAGEMENT

ALSO AVAILABLE FROM KOGAN PAGE

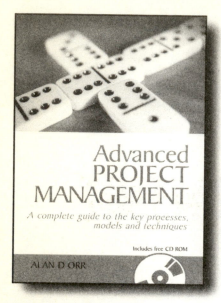

£25.00 0 7494 4094 5
Hardback with CD-ROM 248 pages

£22.50 0 7494 4186 0
Paperback 256 pages

£24.95 0 7494 3965 3
Paperback with CD-ROM 304 pages

£40.00 0 7494 3694 8
Hardback 368 pages

For further information on how to order, please visit

www.kogan-page.co.uk

KOGAN
PAGE

project RISK MANAGEMENT

an essential tool for managing and controlling projects

D van Well-Stam
F Lindenaar
S van Kinderen
B van den Bunt

KOGAN
PAGE

London and Sterling, VA

Publisher's note

Every possible effort has been made to ensure that the information contained in this book is accurate at the time of going to press, and the publishers and authors cannot accept responsibility for any errors or omissions, however caused. No responsibility for loss or damage occasioned to any person acting, or refraining from action, as a result of the material in this publication can be accepted by the editor, the publisher or any of the authors.

First published in Dutch in the Netherlands in 2003 as *Risicomanagement voor projecten* by Het Spectrum
First published in English in Great Britain and the United States in 2004 by Kogan Page Limited.

120 Pentonville Road	22883 Quicksilver Drive	658.404
London N1 9JN	Sterling VA 20166–2012	w447
United Kingdom	USA	c.1
www.kogan-page.co.uk		

© Daniëlla van Well-Stam, Fianne Lindenaar, Suzanne van Kinderen and Bouke van den Bunt, Het Spectrum, translated into English by Allison Klein, 2003, 2004

ISBN 0 7494 4275 1

British Library Cataloguing-in-Publication Data

A CIP record for this book is available from the British Library.

Library of Congress Cataloging-in-Publication Data

Well-Stam, Daniella van
   [Risico management voor projecten. English]
   Project risk management : an essential tool for managing and controlling projects / Daniella van Well-Stam, F. Lindenaar, S. Van Kinderen.
      p. cm.
   ISBN 0-7494-4275-1
   1. Project management. 2. Risk management. I. Lindenaar, F. (Fianne). II. Kinderen, S. van (Suzanne). III. Title. HD69.P75W4513 2004
658.4'04--dc22

2004009945

Typeset by Saxon Graphics Ltd, Derby
Printed and bound in Great Britain by Creative Print and Design (Wales), Ebbw Vale

Contents

About the authors

Over the last few years, the authors of this book have amassed a tremendous amount of experience in performing risk analyses and implementing risk management techniques within projects. Two of the authors are employed by the RISMAN Project Bureau of the Dutch Ministry of Public Works Building Services (Bouwdienst Rijkswaterstaat), and the other two are employed by the consultancy firm Twynstra Gudde. All of the authors frequently work together on assignments and have expertise in the following areas:

- performing risk analyses;
- providing training programmes in the area of risk analysis and management (varying from one-day workshops to three-day courses);
- providing consultancy services on the implementation of risk management;
- coaching project leaders and project managers to enable them to perform risk analyses independently;
- developing products related to risk analysis and risk management.

Bouke van den Bunt studied Civil Engineering at TU (Technical University) Delft. Since 1994 he has been employed at the Bouwdienst Rijkswaterstaat (Building Services at the Dutch Ministry of Public Works) in the field of risk analysis and risk management. He has been the Director of the RISMAN Project Bureau since 2000.

Suzanne van Kinderen studied Civil Engineering at TU Delft. Since 1997 she has worked as a consultant at Twynstra Gudde in Amersfoort where she is active in the field of project management within infrastructures, specializing in risk management for major infrastructure and industrial projects.

Fianne Lindenaar studied Civil Engineering to higher technical school level and continued to study Civil Engineering and Management at the University of Twente. Since 1997 she has been employed at the Bouwdienst Rijkswaterstaat as a risk analysis specialist and at the RISMAN Project Bureau since 1999.

Daniella van Well-Stam studied Business Administration at the Erasmus University in Rotterdam. She has been employed at Twynstra Gudde in Amersfoort since 1995 in the field of risk analysis and risk management. Her speciality lies primarily in major infrastructure projects.

Foreword

When managing a project, you get one chance to get it right. Ideally, you get it right the first time. Unfortunately, newspapers are full of reports of failed projects, projects that have got out of hand or even those that have come to a standstill.

The fact is that it is far from simple to successfully manage a large and complex project. Nearly every person involved, and even those on the outside, operates using his or her own set of criteria for success. Each project is unique, involving individuals who are new to the project and to the circumstances pertaining to it.

A project, therefore, is never without risks. Often we prefer not to see these risks because we have irrational, political or even emotional arguments for completing the project. This does not mean that the risks will not arise, but that those involved in the project will have to go to great lengths after the fact to hide, play down or cope with the setbacks and disappointments. Performing risk analysis and management beforehand is actually necessary to every project, but unfortunately this is not typical.

In writing this book, the authors have made their rich experience in risk analysis and management accessible for anyone who is receptive to the idea of discovering the risks involved in his or her project beforehand. This book is also valuable for those willing to take appropriate measures in order to prevent, avoid, reduce, eliminate or accept these risks by analysing them and their consequences.

Anyone who genuinely plans to manage his or her project successfully will benefit from the succinct descriptions of the methods for risk analysis and management described in this book.

Gert Wijnen
Loenen

Preface

In addition to the project-based approach, for years now there has been a tendency toward focusing explicit attention on risk management in the control of projects.

Since 1995 the RISMAN (RISkMANagement) method for performing risk analysis has been available. This method was developed through a cooperative effort organized among a number of organizations.* In 1999 adjustments were made and the method was expanded to include risk management.

In recent years a great deal of experience has been gained using risk analysis to manage and control projects. At the RWS (Rijkswaterstaat – Ministry of Public Works), and in particular since the RISMAN Project Bureau was established at the Ministry's Building Services office, various project managers within the Ministry of Transport have been providing advice and support in this area. In the process, a tremendous amount of knowledge has been acquired, for example in the practical performance of risk analyses and the implementation of risk management in project organizations. In addition, the methodology and the knowledge gained have proved their applicability to the organization of major sporting events, construction projects and ICT projects.

The authors of this book (employed at the RISMAN Project Bureau and Twynstra Gudde) have acquired substantial experience in the performance of risk analyses and the implementation of risk management within projects. It is their opinion that the application of the method can contribute to better control over every type of project, and for this reason they have decided to write this book to share the knowledge and experience they have acquired.

This book is intended for anyone who is interested in the manner in which risk management may be applied within projects. Although the examples chosen are primarily set in the authors' specific field – the infrastructure sector – the reader will easily be able to incorporate these concepts into his or her own specific situation. Besides, every project involves uncertainties, regardless of the project's content.

The authors would like to thank the project directors of the projects included in this book for their cooperation. The authors are also grateful to Gert Wijnen, co-author of the successful book, *Projectmatig Werken (The Project-based Approach)*, for reading the text and providing them with valuable feedback, and to Arno Willems, a fellow colleague at the RISMAN Project Bureau, for his commentary on the description of quantitative risk analysis.

Note

* The RISMAN method was developed through cooperation between the RWS Bouwdienst, RWS Zuid-Holland, Railinfrabeheer (railway infrastructure management), Twynstra Gudde, TU Delft and the Rotterdam Public Works Department.

1

Introduction

In projects, things often turn out differently than we expect. Sometimes this works in our favour, but often the opposite is true. 'Suddenly' a permit will not be granted on time or losses occur within the project. In order to anticipate these types of events, or to take control over setbacks, it is not sufficient to take action after the fact, but instead to do whatever is necessary to prevent these things from happening. Risk management is a structured form of risk control that unearths possible problems early on, and thus ensures that the project will be better managed.

This book describes the ways in which risk analysis and risk management may be applied within projects. Each chapter will also examine real-life examples of applications of risk analysis and risk management within a number of projects.

We define risk management as follows: *the entire set of activities and measures that are aimed at dealing with risks in order to maintain control over a project.* Risk management is:

- Nothing new. Everyone takes risk into consideration in his or her daily life. A simple example is crossing the street. People do not cross the street without having first looked left and right. Likewise, every project manager or employee also takes risk into consideration in his or her daily work. Many decisions are based upon evaluating the alternatives related to risks. This often occurs implicitly. The strength of risk management lies in providing explicit and structured insight into risks, as well as the ability to take those risks that are preying on people's minds and make them explicit and capable of being discussed.

- Anticipating. The strength of risk management lies in being able to think ahead about all of the things that could possibly go wrong in a project. In this way, measures can be taken to prevent or control the things that might go wrong so that one is able to do more than simply react to something when it goes awry. This involves identifying and taking control over future events.
- Customizing to each project. The method described in this book for risk analysis and risk management is not a strait-jacket in which there is only one proper way of doing things. How the risk analysis is performed and the way in which customized interpretation is applied to the risk management depends, among other things, on the size of the project, the phase of the project and the degree to which the project and its context are dynamic, complex and risky. The analysis may vary from a somewhat rapid, global means of identifying risks to an extensive quantitative risk analysis. The differences will be discussed in depth in this book.

WHY RISK MANAGEMENT?

Risk management provides support for attempts to gain better control over a project when it comes to time (planning/schedules), money (estimates), quality, information and organization. It does this by giving thought beforehand to the undesirable future events or outcomes that might occur in a project, so that decisions may be made to take action early on in order to prevent or reduce the impact of these events.

Risk management can help to:

- promote an uninterrupted progression of the activities within a project and, by implementing the appropriate measures, remove any interruptions as quickly as possible should they occur;
- instil confidence in the project, in third parties, and in the project team itself;

- promote communication within the project;
- support the decision-making process within a project.

So why isn't risk management applied to every project? There are a number of reasons. First, this may be because those involved are not familiar with risk management, and so are not aware of what it has to offer. Second, some people do not relish being forced to recognize the existence of risk. Risk analysis is seen by some as a means of judging the performance of individuals: 'If risks can turn up in my work, then I am obviously not a good manager.' However, we use risk management to try to look ahead and it is therefore not a judgement of events after the fact.

A third reason often offered for not engaging in risk management is that it costs money. It is obvious that risk management and the implementation of control measures involve costs. It is, however, much more difficult to determine precisely how much it will yield. Take travel insurance, for example. You have been on holiday, and nothing bad happened. Did you take out a travel insurance policy for nothing? It has offered you the security that if something should happen, any costs you incur as a result would be compensated.

Finally, companies and organizations often argue that they really do not have the time or capacity to engage in risk management.

In this book, we hope to show that the strength of risk management lies in providing explicit and structured insight into risks, and that it does not have to be too time-consuming. It is possible to gain a clear picture of the risks involved within a project quite quickly.

WHAT IS RISK MANAGEMENT?

Risk management is a cyclical process that must be repeated regularly during the course of a project.

Risk management begins with an analysis of the risks. With the aid of risk analysis, insight into the risks within a project can be gained systematically and the (effects of the) measures used to approach these risks can be evaluated.

A one-off identification of risks through a risk analysis is, however, not enough. Projects are constantly changing and evolving, and risks may either be overcome or decrease as a result of measures being implemented, and new risks might rear their heads. So risks have to be monitored on a regular basis and controlled. The implementation of risk management means building this process into the very fibre of the project itself. The cyclical nature of risk management is illustrated in Figure 1.1.

For what types of projects can it be used?

Risk management may be applied to every type of project, large or small, short or long term, independent of the results to be achieved by the project. The manner in which risk management is applied is, however, dependent upon the nature of the project, the people involved, and the desired results. Risk analysis and risk management for major railway projects such as the High Speed Line South (HSL-Zuid) or the Betuwe Line differ significantly from those activities involved in the construction of a bicycle path by the district council, for example.

At which point in the project can it be used?

Both risk analysis and risk management may be performed from the moment that it becomes clear what the outcome of the

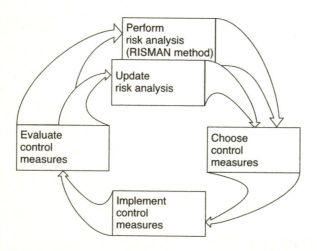

Figure 1.1 The cyclical nature of risk management

project should be, and once the means of achieving it (and the activities involved in doing so) have been identified in broad terms. This starts once the initiation phase has been completed. It is crucial that those involved are aware of the project risks from the initial phase onwards.

The nature of the risks varies according to the phase of the project. If the project is still in the early stages, then many of the risks will involve decision-making. In this phase, risk analysis for the total project is often accompanied by scenario thinking, where the risks are identified using various scenario alternatives so that a balanced evaluation may be made based in part on these risks.

As the project progresses, the risks will be formulated at an increasingly detailed level and will relate more to, for example, the composition of the project team, the method used for contracts (if contracting out is relevant), and the market approach and method employed. Ultimately, those involved in the project will be faced with the risks involved in the execution phase.

RISK MANAGEMENT WITHIN A PROJECT-BASED APPROACH

Risk management is a tool which, within the framework of the project-based approach (Wijnen, Renes and Storm, 2000), can play a supporting role in gaining better control over a project. A number of control aspects are encapsulated in the concept of the project-based approach: time, money, quality, information and organization. Control over the project may be exercised via these five factors. The project-based approach offers tools to help maintain control over the project, but there are always setbacks: local residents who object to plans, a new political policy or a lack of skills among the project employees. With the aid of risk analysis, it is possible to anticipate future deviations, but risk management should not be seen as a sixth control factor.

The relationship between risk, risk management and the project-based approach is illustrated in Figure 1.2.

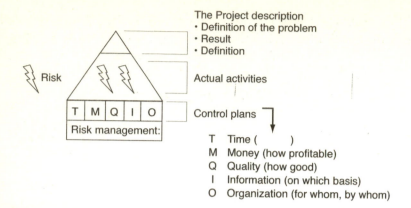

The Project description
• Definition of the problem
• Result
• Definition

Actual activities

Control plans

T   Time (   )
M   Money (how profitable)
Q   Quality (how good)
I   Information (on which basis)
O   Organization (for whom, by whom)

Figure 1.2 Relationship of risk management and the project-based approach

NOT JUST SETBACKS

Although this book primarily focuses on the negative aspects of risks and their prevention, windfalls may also occur in projects. The method described in this book can also be used for identifying opportunities. These are actually also uncertain future events, the only difference being that the resulting consequences have positive effects on the outcome of the project.

It is also the case that what is a risk for one person may be an opportunity for another. It depends entirely on from whose point of view the project is being judged.

HOW TO USE THIS BOOK

We have written this book for project leaders and risk analysts who are interested in applying risk analysis and risk management within projects. By using this book, the reader can gain insights into the manner in which risk analyses may be carried out as well as the applications for risk analysis and risk management.

This book may also serve as a resource for clients and project leaders who, by applying the concepts of risk management, aim to gain better control over their project.

The book is effectively in two parts: analysing risks (risk analysis) and controlling risks (risk management), as shown in Figure 1.3.

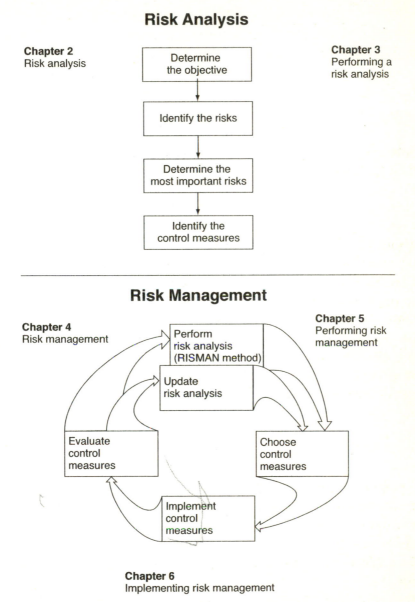

Figure 1.3 The cyclical nature of risk management, and the structure of this book.

The section on risk analysis describes the manner in which it can be customized in terms of its interpretation, and which factors play a role in this process.

In the section on risk management, attention is focused on the step from risk analysis to risk management, the way in which risk management can be performed, and the ways in which risk management can be implemented within a project organization.

The chapters conclude with a number of examples from several actual projects:

- Hogesnelheidslijn Zuid (HSL-ZUID) (High-Speed Line South);
- Betuweroute;
- Maaswerken;
- Westerschelde Tunnel;
- Euro 2000.

The projects are described below.

CASE STUDIES

The Dutch High-Speed Line
In 2007, the Netherlands will become part of the Trans-European Network of high-speed rail links. The HSL will link Amsterdam and Rotterdam to Antwerp, Brussels and Paris. A quick sprint from Amsterdam to Rotterdam will take no more than 35 minutes. Cities such as London (3 hrs 43 mins) and Barcelona (7 hrs 15 mins) will be brought a lot closer. The HSL will provide a growing number of travellers with an environmentally friendly alternative to driving or flying. Holland as a whole and its western conurbation the Randstad in particular will be more accessible. Between 6 and 7 million people are expected to use the High-Speed Line annually for domestic journeys, with about the same number choosing it for their international travel needs.

Decisions to link infrastructure projects of this size and complexity are not taken lightly. The first plans for the Dutch HSL were made in 1986; the final decision in 2000 to start building the Dutch HSL was preceded by a large number of exploratory studies and an exhaustive public consultation procedure.

Figure 1.4 High speed train

The most important procedures were the Key Planning Decision (KPD) and the procedure called for under the Infrastructure (Planning Procedures) Act. During the course of the KPD procedure (1991–97), studies were conducted to determine whether the construction of a high-speed line was feasible and, if so, how such a task might best be accomplished. Once the government and parliament had decided to go ahead with the project, it became possible for the Infrastructure (Planning Procedures) Act procedure to commence in 1997. This further elaborated on the preferred route identified in the KPD and also provided those likely to be affected by the line with several opportunities to make their views known and to lodge any objections.

Following the evaluation of objections by the Council of State, the final version of the Route Decision became irrevocable during 2000. In the same year, the first contracts were awarded and initial preparations for construction were made. Thousands of permits and licences were required for the construction of the HSL: tree felling permits, drainage permits and building permits to name just three. The budget totals approximately €5.3 billion.

The Dutch High-Speed Line from Amsterdam to the Belgian border is a Ministry of Transport, Public Works and Water Management project. In 2007, the HSL Project Organization (part of the Directorate-General for Public Works and Water Management (Rijkswaterstaat)) is scheduled to deliver a completely new rail system: a comprehensive package comprising both infrastructure and trains.

Working alongside government employees in the project organization are individuals employed in the private-sector. The project organization also regularly employs the services of external consultants. The project organization is divided into one central unit and a number of regional project offices.

For the construction of the High-Speed Line, the project organization has awarded contracts to a number of private-sector building contractors. The substructure is let in six primary contracts for design, construction and maintenance. For the design, building, finance and maintenance of HSL's rail systems (superstructure), an infrastructure provider has been contracted for a 25-year period. Once the line has been completed, the infrastructure provider will be paid an annual fee for the use of HSL rail services. Finally, a train operating consortium has been contracted for providing domestic and international passenger train services for the HSL.

The route of the Dutch High-Speed Line is a gentle curve approximately 100 kilometres long running from Amsterdam to the Belgian border. There are no level crossings and, wherever possible, the new line runs parallel to existing railway lines or motorways (A4 and A16).

In Amsterdam and Rotterdam and near Breda, the line is linked to the existing network so that trains can access stations. The Hague will have a fast shuttle link to the High-Speed Line. The entire route is a succession of 170 structures: tunnels, submerged tunnels, underpasses, bridges, flyovers, sunken and semi-sunken concrete U-boxes and an elevated section. The most striking yet 'hidden' construction segment of the HSL is the 7 kilometre-long bored tunnel under the 'Green Heart' of the Netherlands. Another key construction feature is the bridge over the Hollandsch Diep, which, at 1.2 kilometres, is the longest bridge over water between Amsterdam and Paris.

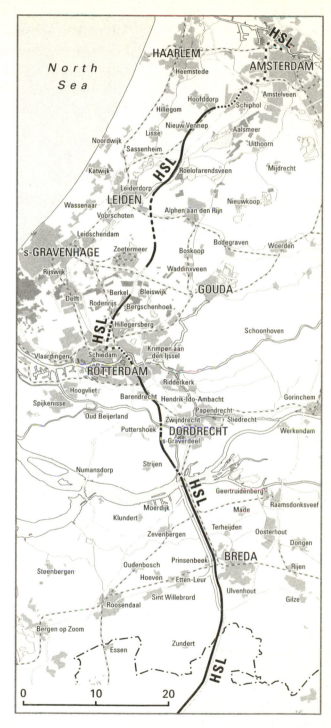

Figure 1.5 Route of Dutch HSL

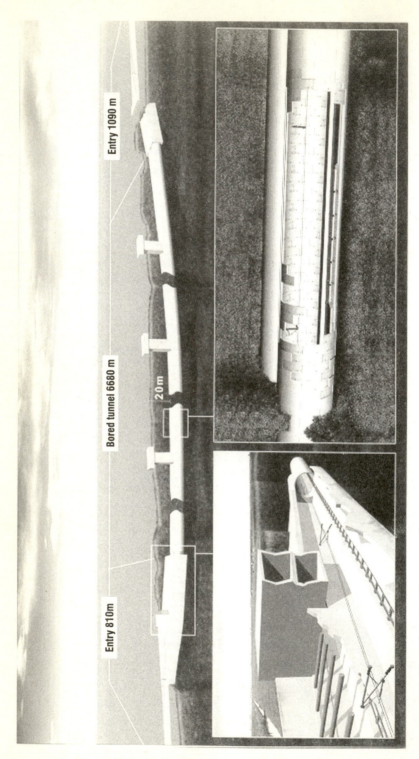

Figure 1.6 Bored tunnel groene hart

Some facts and figures on the High-Speed Line:

- total length of line: 100 kilometres;
- construction: piled concrete slab track;
- 25 per cent of the route will be at ground level, the remaining 75 per cent consisting of approximately 170 elevated or sunken structures: flyovers, underpasses, embankments, cuttings, four tunnels and a major bridge over water;
- cost: €5.3 billion (at 2000 prices);
- opening: 2007;
- speed: up to 300 kph;
- power supply: 25kV;
- safety: Europe's most modern rail safety system.

Betuweroute

The Betuweroute is a 160-kilometre double-track railway line exclusively intended for freight transport between the Port of Rotterdam and the German border at Zevenaar-Emmerich.

Production and distribution represent the lion's share of the European economy. Consumers are developing more specific demands, leading to a new worldwide flow of goods. For the European mainland, the port of Rotterdam is an important gateway for all sorts of goods such as raw materials, semi-manufactures and consumer goods. The new railway line will be the backbone of Dutch freight rail and will provide the Netherlands with a valuable connection to the European freight rail network. The Betuweroute will be able to process 10 freight trains an hour in each direction, travelling at a maximum speed of 120 kph.

The decision process has taken years. Important milestones were the publication of the Key Planning Decision (KPD) in 1994, the granting of permission by parliament for construction of the route in 1995, and the adoption of the Route Decision in 1996.

The track of the Betuweroute encompasses much more than just rails and overhead wires. Eighty per cent of the railway line is bundled with the A15 motorway. Anyone travelling from the sea to Zevenaar would encounter a total of 130 structures including bridges, viaducts and junctions along the way. Nine of these structures are quite remarkable in size. The new Dintelhaven Rail Bridge is located between the Maasvlakte and the Botlek.

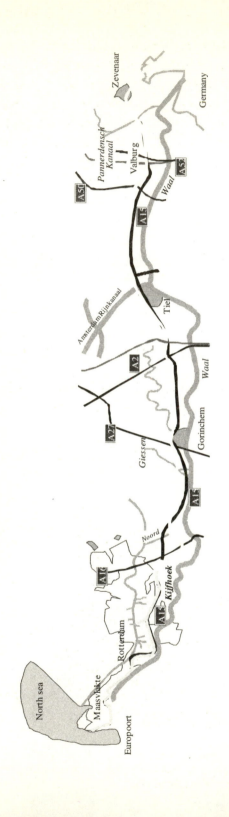

Figure 1.7 Line of Betuweroute

The Botlek Rail Tunnel, built by an innovative boring method, is located a bit further inland. The traveller then passes the enlarged and modernized shunting yards of Kijfhoek. In Barendrecht, the track disappears beneath a multifunctional roofing structure measuring 1.5 kilometres in length. The largest structure along the route is the Sophia Rail Tunnel, spanning over 8 kilometres. In Giessenlanden the track runs underneath the Giessen River through a tunnel. The town of Valburg is home to a Central Interchange Point (CIP). A tunnel will be bored beneath the Pannerdensch Canal, and in Zevenaar the Betuweroute will also run through a tunnel. All of these structures are being built to minimize the Betuweroute's impact on the surrounding areas and to create a fast route passed waterways and junctions.

The commissioning party for the construction of the Betuweroute is the Department of Public Works (Rijkswaterstaat) of the Ministry of Transport, Public Works and Water Management.

Prorail (the former Rail Infra Management) has been commissioned to construct the new railway line. To carry out the

Figure 1.8 Sophia Rail Tunnel
Source: Project Organisation Betuweroute, photographer: Ronald Tilleman (Rotterdam), reproduced with permission

complex set of tasks with optimal efficiency, the Betuweroute Project has offices at various locations throughout the country. The Rijkswaterstaat's main offices are located in The Hague. The commissionee, Railinfrabeheer, has its offices in Utrecht. In addition, Railinfrabeheer has two regional offices (one for the province of South Holland located in Barendrecht, and another in Tiel for the province of Gelderland) and numerous site offices along the Betuweroute's 160-kilometre track. The budget totals approximately €4.8 billion.

Some facts and figures on the Betuweroute:

- length: 160 kilometres;
- bundling with A15: 95 kilometres;
- number of tunnels: 5;
- number of viaducts/bridges: 130;
- number of overhead cable portals: 5,600;
- number of points: 155;
- volume of sand: 16 million m^3;
- construction time in people-years: 20,000;
- design speed: 120 kph maximum;
- capacity: 10 trains per hour in each direction.

Maaswerken

The Meuse River (or 'Maas' in Dutch) traverses the province of Limburg and parts of Noord-Brabant and Gelderland. This river must remain controllable, regardless of the volume of water it discharges. For this reason, measures such as widening and deepening the riverbed had to be considered. In accordance with both Dutch and international policies, these measures provide more space for rivers for discharge and for ecological recovery. These plans for the Meuse are being engineered and implemented by the Maaswerken project organization together with the cooperation of the Ministry of Transport, Public Works and Water Management, the Province of Limburg and the Ministry of Agriculture, Nature Management and Fisheries. The plans for the Meuse will be completed in 2015.

The Maaswerken plans are based on the national 'Delta Plan for the Main Rivers'. The decision to execute this plan was made as a result of the flooding that occurred in 1993 and 1995.

Figure 1.9 High water in Meuse area, in 1993
Source: Rijkswaterstaat, Geo-Information and ICT Department

The project's primary aim is to provide more adequate protection by reducing the probability of flooding to 1:250 per annum (this figure equals a discharge of 3,900 cubic metres per second). To achieve this goal, additional measures will have to be taken such as the building of embankments and enlarging the riverbed to accommodate floodwaters. In addition to the specific goals set for the Grensmaas (Border Meuse) and the Zandmaas/ Maasroute (Sand Meuse/Meuse Route) projects, flood control is the main objective of the Maaswerken. The budget for Sand Meuse and Border Meuse totals approximately €550 million.

The plans for the Sand Meuse/Meuse Route subproject were adopted by the Provincial States of Limburg and the State Secretary of Transport, Public Works and Water Management on

Figure 1.10 Maaswerken projects

14 March 2002, following which preparations for the execution of the project were set in motion. Work will begin in early 2004.

The objectives for the Sand Meuse/Meuse Route are:

- annual flood protection of 1:250 behind the quays (Sand Meuse);
- improvement in the waterway (Meuse Route);
- limited nature development.

History:

1991	Start Meuse Route
1995	Start Sand Meuse (motivation: floods of 1993 and 1995); merger of both subprojects
March 2002	Finalization of plans (adopted within the Planning Procedures Decree for the Sand Meuse/Meuse Route and the Provincial Planning Scheme for Limburg – Sand Meuse Supplement)
April 2004	Start work
December 2015	Work complete (according to the current schedule)

The plans for the Border Meuse have been in place for over 10 years and the end of the planning phase is now in sight. At present, those involved in the project are waiting for a final decision from the European Commission on the tender variant chosen (self-fulfilment). Later, the Provincial States of Limburg will make an announcement on the plans, according to which work will start in 2005.

Objectives of the Border Meuse:

• annual flood protection of 1:250 behind the quays;
• creation of at least 1,000 hectares of new natural environment;
• gravel extraction;
• the intended objectives should be realized in a budget-neutral manner.

History

1995	Delta Plan Major Rivers with the objective of annual flood protection of 1:250 behind the quays
1998	EIS (Environmental Impact Statement) and Design-Regional Plan, Border Meuse (decision delayed)
2001	Final Plan, Border Meuse
2003	Design-Provincial Development Plan and EIS Border Meuse: participation and decision-making
2005	Start work

The project organization, De Maaswerken, employs approximately 100 people in river engineering, finance, communication, legal affairs, archaeology and land management. These individuals come from a variety of organizations: the Limburg Directorate, Civil Engineering Division and other departments within the Rijkswaterstaat (the Directorate-General for Public Works and Water Management); the Province of Limburg; the Ministry of Agriculture, Nature Management and Fisheries; and others.

In addition to these agencies, many other local, provincial and national authorities and NGOs are involved. The final responsibility for the project lies with the Ministry of Transport, Public Works and Water Management.

Westerschelde Tunnel
The Westerschelde Tunnel is a bored tunnel 6.6 kilometres long located in the south western region of the Netherlands between Central Zeeland (island region) and the mainland area of Zeeland Flanders. The tunnel forms the final link in a chain of fixed shore connections between the various islands of the province of Zeeland. The construction of the tunnel means the end of the two ferry connections, Kruiningen-Perkpolder and Vlissingen-Breskens, and the 'crossing' over the Westerschelde is now considerably quicker as well as being available 24 hours a day.

The history of the development of the fixed shore connection is a rather long one, characterized by many years of (political) discussions. In the late 1980s, an initiative on the part of the Province of Zeeland led to a decision to construct a tunnel. In 1995, the NV Westerscheldetunnel (public limited company) was established, in which the state (Ministries of Transport, Public Works and Water Management and of Finance) holds 95 per cent of the shares and the Province of Zeeland the remaining 5 per cent.

The NV Westerscheldetunnel is the principal commissioning the construction of the tunnel, which was begun in 1999. In 2003 the tunnel, including a toll plaza and approach roads, was completed. The construction costs were approximately €750 million; the total cost (including development and maintenance)

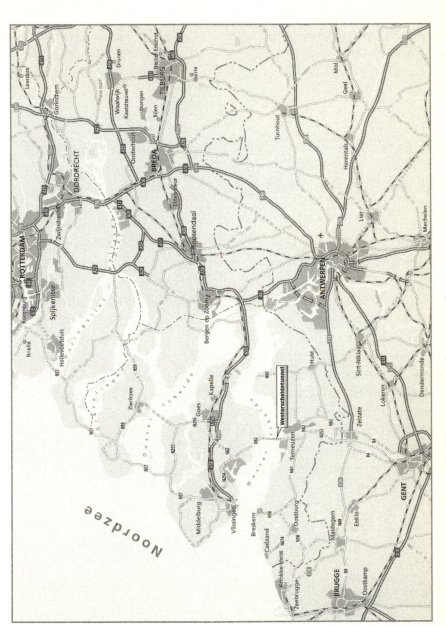

Figure 1.11 Geographical location of the tunnel

will amount to €1.3 billion over a 30-year period. Of this, 40 per cent will be financed by income from tolls and 60 per cent by state and provincial subsidies. The NV is responsible for the operation of the tunnel. The shareholders will see a return on their investment within 30 years. After 30 years, the NV will transfer the Westerschelde Tunnel to the state for a token amount and its use will be free of charge. From that point onwards, the state will pay for the costs of the tunnel's operation.

The Westerschelde Tunnel comprises two tunnel tubes, each 11 metres in diameter, and connected to one another by 25 transverse links measuring roughly 12 metres in length. The tunnel wall was constructed using ring elements. At each end of the tunnel, the distance between the tunnel tubes has been reduced to approximately 7 metres so that the width of the roads leading into the tunnel could be restricted. Each tunnel tube comprises two traffic lanes each 3.5 metres in width. A cable channel has been installed under the road surface. Using a miniature vehicle, maintenance mechanics can negotiate this channel to gain access to any point along the 6.6-kilometre tunnel.

The construction of the tunnel was a technically unique project. Most of the tunnels in Europe, particularly those that have been bored, are built in hard, rocky material. Never before in Western Europe had a tunnel so long and so deep been bored through relatively soft substrates such as sand and clay. The deepest point lies 60 metres below NAP (Normal Amsterdam Level – sea level). In spite of this depth, the gradient at any point in the tunnel is never steeper than 4.5 per cent. A bored tunnel does not have the disadvantages of a bridge (limited clearance for ships) or those of a traditional, submerged tunnel (anchors may damage it) and ultimately proves to be the least expensive solution.

A total of 6,600 tunnel rings were made for the tunnel, 3,300 for each tube. Each tunnel ring is composed of seven segments and a 'keystone'. Each ring is 2 metres wide. The segments and keystones were constructed in a purpose-built concrete factory located at the construction site near Terneuzen (in Zeeland Flanders).

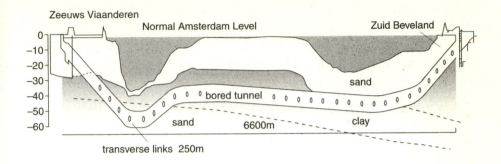

Figure 1.12 Longitudinal cross-section

The transverse links, 2 metres high and 1.5 metres wide, serve as emergency exits and as such are essential for safety; the related costs represent 10 per cent of the construction budget. Under normal circumstances, the doors leading to the transverse links are bolted shut, but in the event of an emergency they are automatically unlatched and one may walk to the other tunnel tube if necessary. Emergency workers may also travel this route to reach the scene of an accident. During construction, the soil between the tunnel tubes was frozen (to -35 degrees Celsius!) so that the transverse links could be built. Prior to the construction of the Westerschelde Tunnel, this freezing technique had never been applied on such a large scale.

Some facts and figures on the Westerschelde Tunnel:

- tunnel length: 6.6 kilometres;
- number of boring machines: 2;
- deepest point: 60 metres below sea level;
- pressure at the deepest point: 7 bar;
- number of tunnel segments: 53,000;
- weight of tunnel segments: 11,000 kilograms each;
- boring slurry removed: 1.5 million m³;
- width of tunnel rings: 2 metres.

Euro 2000

The European Football Championship, played between European national teams, is regarded as the third most impor-

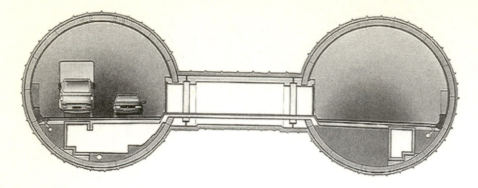

Figure 1.13 Tunnel tubes with transverse link

tant sporting event in the world, after the Olympic Games and the World Football Championships for national teams.

Euro 2000 was held from 10 June (opening match: Turkey-Portugal) to 2 July (final: France-Italy: 2–1). Four of the eight stadiums that hosted the tournament were in the Netherlands, in the cities of Amsterdam, Rotterdam, Eindhoven and Arnhem, with the remaining four in Belgium (Brussels, Liège, Bruges and Charleroi). The tournament was the first of its size to be organized by two countries.

The tournament's mission was:

> With Euro 2000, we hope to demonstrate that football is a sport without borders. We will do this by spreading the message that cooperation is the key to success starting with the successful joint organization composed of two countries that was behind the European Football Championships for national teams. The main aim of our activities is the promotion of football, youth and cooperation.

The tournament's main objectives were:

1. successful cooperation across borders;
2. a financially sound event;
3. good organization of the event (at a minimum, comparable to that of Euro 96); and
4. a public success.

Figure 1.14 shows a simplified version of the 'Network of objective of efforts' for Euro 2000.

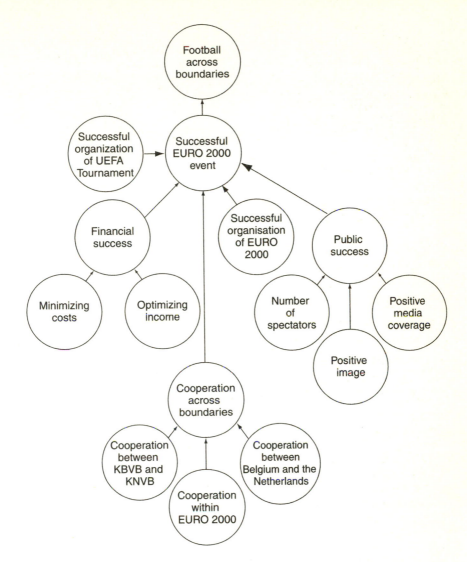

Figure 1.14 Objectives of Euro 2000

Several parties were directly involved in the organization of Euro 2000. The relationships between them were complex, mainly as a result of the position and role of UEFA as the holder of the legal and commercial rights. UEFA acted as principal and Euro 2000 as contractor; the relationship between Euro 2000 and UEFA was the axis around which the other parties involved were positioned. Other parties directly involved were:

- the KBVB (Royal Belgian Football Association) via the specially established Belfoot 2000 Foundation;
- the KNVB (Royal Dutch Football Association);
- EBU and FORTO 2000 (host broadcaster);
- the commercial agency ISL;
- sponsors and suppliers;
- stadiums;
- government bodies (national, regional and local).

The Euro 2000 Foundation comprised a board as well as an office. The office was run by a director, and the upper level of the organization remained constant throughout the process. The organizational structure within the office changed along with each new phase of the project. Initially, the office was small and the organization was quite simple and informal. Later, the organization grew and became more function-oriented and complex. During the realization phase, the organization grew to be quite large (approximately 2,000 members of staff) and activities became highly decentralized. At that point, the tasks, responsibilities and powers were primarily assigned to the eight local organizations instead of being delegated to the central body. In the final, post-delivery phase, the organization returned to its initial smaller, simpler form.

The total Euro 2000 project was divided into approximately 180 subprojects. Various aspects were specified for each subproject: objective and result to be achieved (quality), duration (planning), finance (income and expenses), activities to be performed and required capacity (effort involved).

The project began in 1993 and the event's ultimate dates influenced the set-up of the planning. The planning of the subprojects and the activities associated with them then followed from this design. Figure 1.15 provides an outline of the planning as well as an indication of the decision documents and the moments when decisions involving these documents were to be made.

Statistics for Euro 2000:

- project duration 8 years, with 4 years of preparation;
- 16 teams and 31 matches in 8 cities and 2 countries;
- over 2,000 employees (including volunteers);

Figure 1.15 Basic planning of Euro 2000

- 5,000 members of the press;
- 900,000 spectators;
- an organization budget of approximately €58 million (excluding stadium construction activities);
- over 1.5 billion TV viewers.

2

Risk analysis

Risk management always begins with the analysis of risks. The manner in which a risk analysis is performed varies from project to project, but regardless of how it is carried out, the result is always an overview of the most important risk factors and the possible measures to control them.

A risk analysis contains the steps shown in Figure 2.1; this chapter discusses the steps.

An important feature of the risk analysis method described in this book is that the risks are identified from the broadest point of view possible. In practice, in performing a risk analysis the accent is frequently placed on one specific aspect of the project, technology for example. Our experience is that risks often stem from primarily non-technical aspects, such as the failure to obtain permits, capacity problems and miscommunication. Various approaches may be used in the process of identifying the risks.

SETTING THE OBJECTIVES OF THE RISK ANALYSIS

This is an extremely important first step and is a determining factor for the manner in which the risk analysis will be interpreted.

To design the risk analysis properly, it is necessary to first answer the following questions:

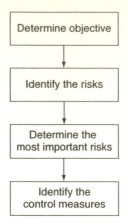

Figure 2.1 Risk analysis

- What do you hope to achieve with the risk analysis?
- Which control aspects does the analysis target?
- Which segment of the project and which phase of the project does the analysis target?
- Is a qualitative or quantitative risk analysis required?
- What type of information is available/usable?

In answering these questions, it is also important to consider from whose perspective the issues are being examined. The success of a project may be defined differently by the various players involved, and so too the potential risks. The success of the project depends upon the person evaluating the risks (see Figure 2.2).

What do you hope to achieve with the risk analysis?

A risk analysis may be used for:

- Improving control over the project. In this case, the risk analysis focuses on providing more insight into the risks that might influence the control aspects of the project. In order to tackle these risks, measures must then be identified.
- Setting priorities. A risk analysis produces insight into the most important (ie, risky) aspects of the project. This allows

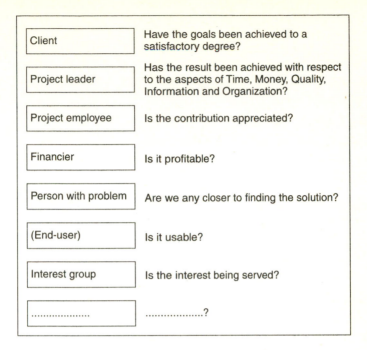

Client	Have the goals been achieved to a satisfactory degree?
Project leader	Has the result been achieved with respect to the aspects of Time, Money, Quality, Information and Organization?
Project employee	Is the contribution appreciated?
Financier	Is it profitable?
Person with problem	Are we any closer to finding the solution?
(End-user)	Is it usable?
Interest group	Is the interest being served?
....	....................?

Figure 2.2 Different perspectives on success

answers to be formulated for questions such as, 'Which aspect requires more attention than others?'

- Support in making a decision. A risk analysis may also be used as a supporting aid in this type of situation. A decision may involve making a choice between various alternatives or for a certain form of contract.
- A (quantitative) basis for the margins for estimates or plans: in this case, a risk analysis is used to demonstrate the feasibility of the plan or estimate. In addition, the level of incidental expenditure may be determined on the basis of the risk analysis. This is only possible by performing a quantitative risk analysis based on an estimate or plans.

In summary, a risk analysis may be used to:

- achieve more control over a project;
- improve the setting of priorities;
- make a well-founded decision;
- obtain a better foundation for an estimate or plan.

Which control aspects does the analysis target?

Once the goal of the risk analysis has been established, the focus of the risk analysis must then be determined. The analysis may target the control aspects (time, money, quality, information and organization), but may also focus on other factors.

In a risk analysis that focuses on time, the relevant risks are those that could lead to delays in the project. Risk analyses targeting quality focus on the risks that threaten the quality of the project's result. Examples of quality aspects include: safety, strength, reliability and maintainability. The risk analysis may also be aimed at multiple control aspects simultaneously.

By establishing which control aspect(s) the risk analysis will focus on, the 'most undesirable event', to use risk analysis terminology, will be determined. This event may be defined as the one that would most displease the client, such as failing to complete the project on time or failing to complete a portion of the project within budget.

In practice, people often ask, 'Why don't you target your analysis on all of these aspects simultaneously; after all, you want to control all of the risks, don't you?' However, one particular aspect is often the decisive one. For example, if you are a project manager and have a budget within which you absolutely must remain, but it would not be the end of the world if the project were completed a month late, then the risk analysis is primarily targeted on costs. This does not mean that the risks of delay are not incorporated into the analysis and, of course, in most cases delays can lead to additional costs, which will then in fact be considered a risk. Conversely, when the project manager has made firm commitments on the completion date of the project and delays lead to high penalties, then the risk analysis will be targeted primarily on those risks that lead to delays.

So, it is not always necessary to target all of the aspects simultaneously in performing a risk analysis.

Which segment of the project and which phase of the project does the analysis target?

In principle, the risk analysis should be able to target every partial result and every phase within the total project. Examples are the examination of the risks for an important tunnel located along a section of the railway, rather than the entire line, and the identification of the risks up to the design stage rather than for all of the project.

Decisions that appear to be favourable in one phase could have a negative consequence in later phases. The risk analysis first targets those risks that could endanger the final result of the project and then focuses on those that threaten the results in particular phases.

The focus of the risk analysis shown in Figure 2.3 is based on the project-based approach phasing process.

The current phase of the project is examined in detail, with a preview of the end result and the follow-up.

Obviously, the further into the future one looks, the less is known about the project and its context. In this case, risk management takes on a different character, much broader in nature and more closely targeted on the greatest (most harmful) risks. In the early stage of a project, the risk analysis is often accompanied by scenario thinking: there are more project results to be defined.

Is a qualitative or quantitative risk analysis required?

Another important question to raise before starting is whether it is preferable to perform a qualitative or quantitative risk analysis. In performing a qualitative analysis, an indication based on size or magnitude is used to determine which risks are the most

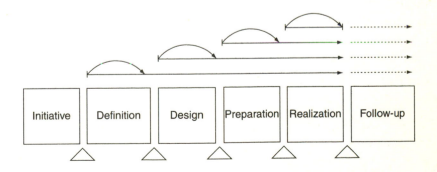

Figure 2.3 Focus of risk management

important. In a quantitative risk analysis, the risks are described in terms of probabilities and consequences. Probabilities are expressed on a scale between zero and one, and the consequences in money, if it involves costs, and in weeks if the analysis involves time. This information will allow calculations of the uncertainty of the total costs or the total time required for the project and the risks can be ranked in order of importance.

The choice between a qualitative and a quantitative risk analysis is initially dependent upon the intended objective of the risk analysis. For example, when the project manager wants to gain insight into the feasibility of the estimate for the project, a quantitative analysis is necessary, for which plans or estimates are required.

Each type of analysis provides different information and thus each is used for a different purpose. To help make an informed choice between quantitative and qualitative analyses, we have listed the most important characteristics of both in Table 2.1.

What type of information is available/usable?

To perform a risk analysis, it needs to be clear what exactly the project entails, in which phase the project is situated, what infor-

Table 2.1 Qualitative and quantitative risk analysis compared

Qualitative risk analysis	Quantitative risk analysis
When to use it – for risk management purposes	*When to use it* – demonstrate/support feasibility of the estimate/schedule – support for the contingency items
Advantages – provides a quick and clear picture of the risks, one that is easily understandable for everyone	*Advantages* – effect of the measures may be mapped out more clearly
Disadvantages – prioritization provides less information	*Disadvantages* – analysis requires a great deal of time and effort – figures/outcomes may take on a life of their own, starting points/ assumptions disappear

mation is available, etc. The degree of detail available on the project will determine the level of detail possible in the outcome of the risk analysis.

To perform a proper risk analysis, it is necessary to have a clear picture of the approach used in the project. The following information will be useful:

- project plan;
- schedule;
- cost estimates;
- quality plan;
- information plan;
- organizational diagram or plan (how the project is organized internally);
- the programme of results for the project, possibly including an outline of the partial results;
- a chart of the context (the players with a role in the project).

IDENTIFY THE RISKS

This step involves a description of how the risks may be identified for a project. The definition of a risk will be explored as well as the thinking model, the manner in which risks may be named and the manner in which the results may be represented.

This step involves taking stock and making lists; it closely resembles a brainstorming process. A thinking model is used, as described below. The main rule is that selection and/or prioritization of activities does not take place in this phase, so as to avoid any interference with the brainstorming and broad list-making process.

What is a risk?

Before going into more depth on the manner in which risks may be identified, it is important to have an accurate picture of precisely what a risk is and how it may best be formulated. There are many definitions of a risk and they are often used interchangeably. We define a risk as an event that may or may not occur and can lead to:

- higher costs;
- extension of the project;
- failure to satisfy specified quality requirements or norms;
- failure to satisfy specified information requirements or norms;
- failure to satisfy specified organizational requirements or norms.

Probability and consequences may be identified within this definition. The probability aspect is reflected in the statement 'an event that may or may not occur' – it may not happen. Therefore, something that is certain is not a risk. It is very important to be aware that current bottlenecks or concerns are often labelled as risks.

Consequences indicate where the risk may lead. This book assumes consequences for the control aspects of time, money, quality, information and organization.

The thinking model

The essence of identifying risks is that the project is examined in a systematic manner from many points of view in order to obtain the most complete identification of the risks possible. You will never achieve 100 per cent coverage in this process: it is simply not possible to think of everything beforehand.

The thinking model used is a risk matrix. This matrix is shown in Figure 2.4 and should be seen as a model that you fill in mentally. The project is shown on the vertical axis and the points of view on the horizontal axis. These points of view or approaches serve as an aid in identifying the potential risks for the project. The risk matrix is explained in more depth below.

The vertical axis of the risk matrix: the project

The vertical axis matrix represents that portion of the project that is targeted by the risk analysis: this may be phases, subprojects, milestones or partial results. This axis must be the best possible depiction of the project.

In plotting items along this axis, it is best to assume the set-up of the project as it currently exists.

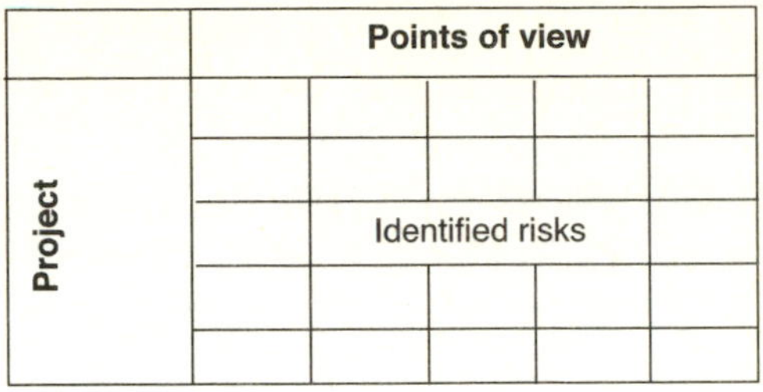

Figure 2.4 Risk matrix

The horizontal axis of the risk matrix: points of view

The horizontal axis serves as a 'trigger' from which the project may be observed in order to identify risks. The horizontal axis encourages people who are charged with the identification of risks to look at the project from various points of view. This process reduces the chance of project 'short-sightedness'. Points of view in infrastructure projects include:

- technical;
- organizational;
- zoning;
- political/administrative;
- legal/legislative;
- financial/economic;
- social/community-related.

Appendix 1 includes a checklist that may be used as an aid in the identification of risks from each point of view.

Experience has taught us that these points of view may be applied to nearly every type of project, although some may be replaced. For example, in ICT projects, technological, legal, environmental, financial and organizational points of view are used. DESTEP (demographic, economic, social, technological, ecological and political) developments can be used as another means of classification for the points of view in making lists of risks.

In addition to points of view, an environmental analysis can also be used when considering the risks involved in a project. In this case, you must first list all of the possible parties who may be involved in the project. To identify the parties, the following questions must be asked (Groote *et al*, 2000):

- Who makes the decisions regarding the project?
- Who will be making use of the results or be affected by their consequences?
- Who will be executing the project?
- Who will be making people, means or expertise available for the project?

Figure 2.5 includes an example of a chart that can be used to show the parties involved. (See Groote *et al*, 2000, for further information on environmental analysis.)

Next, the parties can examine how their impact on the project may lead to risks.

In performing an environmental analysis, in addition to making a list of the interested parties ('stakeholders'), it is also extremely useful to chart related projects. This may involve projects that have a physical relationship with the project for which a risk analysis is being performed, but it may also involve projects that could exert influence in terms of policy.

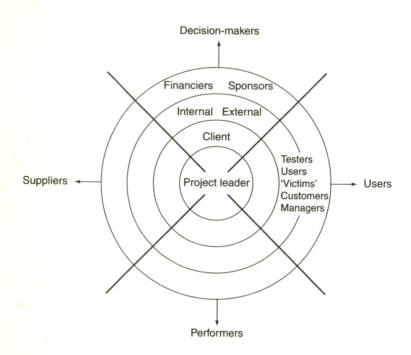

Figure 2.5 The environment

The choice of the design for the thinking model to be used depends on the preferences of those individuals who are listing the risks. We recommended that several different methods are used so as to achieve a sufficient degree of variety.

Formulating a risk

It is crucial to formulate a risk as plainly and concretely as possible so that it becomes clear what could possibly go wrong (undesirable event), as a result of what or whom it can arise (cause) and the areas it can influence (effect or consequence).

The formulation of a risk is made up of cause, event and consequence and is shown in Tables 2.2 and 2.3.

A risk is not a question and must consist of more than one word. A risk must be clearly defined so that when the important risks are established later, everyone will at least have the same picture for each risk. In addition, a well-formulated risk (including cause and effect) provides a basis for establishing control measures.

Imagine that you have bought an old house that needs renovating. Before you start, you carry out a risk analysis: your budget is limited and you need to identify any risks that could lead to additional costs during the renovation.

Structuring a risk

Sometimes it can prove useful to present risks in a structured manner in schematic form. This is particularly practical when

Table 2.2 Risks and consequences

Incorrect formulation	Correct formulation
Concrete decay	Concrete repairs will have to be performed by a specialized company due to unexpected discovery of damage to the foundation from concrete decay
Will the permits be granted on time?	Permits will not be granted on time
The contractor is now charging a higher price	The contractor quotes a higher price (as a result of an overburdened market) than what you had accounted for in your own estimate of the costs

Table 2.3 Risks, causes and effects

Risk	Causes	Effects
Concrete repairs must be performed by a specialized company	Unexpected discovery of concrete decay in the foundation	Additional costs
The permits will not be granted on time	Objections by neighbouring residents to the permits	Delay and additional costs
	Delay in the permit application process due to lack of availability of all of the necessary information	
	Insufficient capacity at agency granting permit	
The contractor is charging a higher price than was expected	Overburdened market Own estimate is of unsatisfactory quality; was estimated too positively	Additional costs
	No margins have been included	
Etc		

your goal is to gain insight into the relationship between risks, causes and effects. Various types of 'pictures' or 'diagrams' can be used for this purpose.

The diagrams are 'thought pictures', models of the complex reality represented schematically. In risk diagrams, the cause and effect relationships are shown as well as the impact that risks and uncertainties have on one another. As a result, it becomes easier to get right to the core of the problem. There are a number of types of diagrams that can be used:

- cause and effect diagrams;
- fault trees;
- event trees;
- influence diagrams.

Cause and effect diagrams

A cause and effect diagram is a schematic rendition of the causes and effects of a risk, which displays the origins of a risk as well as the consequences to which it can lead. For each risk that is identified, the causes and effects are analysed and shown in the diagram.

Figure 2.6 is an example of a cause and effect diagram showing the risks involved in cables and lines within a project.

Fault trees

A fault tree is a schematic representation of causes that can lead to a certain risk (most undesirable event). The purpose of a fault tree is to identify the causes that could lead to this risk. The risk is shown at the top of the fault tree.

Preparing a fault tree is particularly useful when greater insight into the causes of one or more risks is desirable; Figure 2.7 shows an example.

Event trees

An event tree is an aid in analysing the consequences of a specific risk. In this case, the risk is called the initiating event. An event tree shows how this initiating event, in combination with

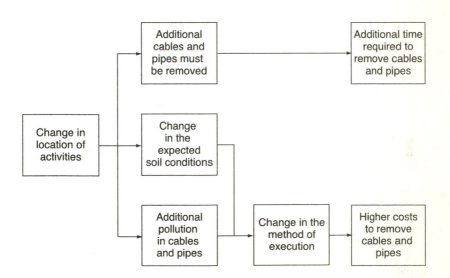

Figure 2.6 A cause and effect diagram

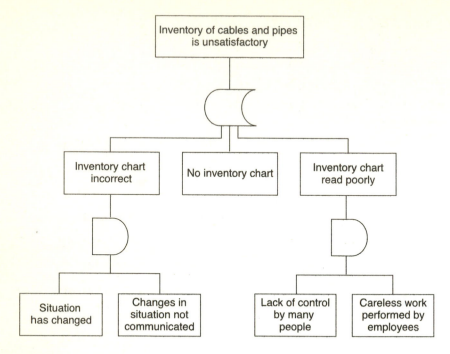

Figure 2.7 A fault tree

subsequent events (or lack thereof), can lead to certain consequences.

Creating an event tree is particularly useful when more insight
into the consequences of one or more risks is the desired result;
Figure 2.8 shows an example.

Influence diagrams

An influence diagram is a graphical representation of the factors
that may have an influence on the control aspects of a project.
These influential factors may be events or decisions. Their relationship with one another is indicated through the use of
arrows. In this way, a complex 'system' may be described in a
relatively compact manner. An example of an influence diagram
is shown in Figure 2.9.

An important difference between the influence diagram and
the other schematic techniques is that the influential factors are
formulated neutrally, which means that no indication is given

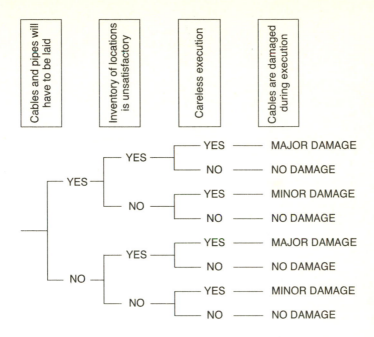

Figure 2.8 An event tree

whether these factors can develop positively or negatively. There are thus no 'real' risks shown in this type of diagram.

DETERMINE THE MOST IMPORTANT RISKS

During the process of identification, a great number of risks may emerge. It is unproductive and most certainly not necessary to focus attention on all of the risks that have been identified. For an average project, a great many risks may quickly emerge. Priority must be given to the most significant.

Because it is very difficult to compare the risks concerning time, money, quality, information and organization and to rank them in order of importance, this step should be carried out separately for each control aspect.

The most important risks can be identified in a qualitative as well as quantitative manner. This chapter describes the qualitative manner of establishing the most important risks (prioritizing). For information on quantitative risk analysis, see Appendix 2.

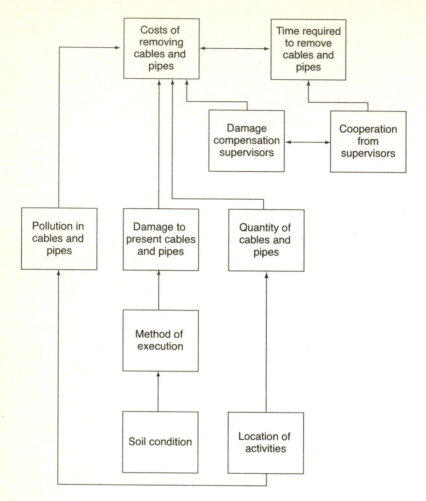

Figure 2.9 An event diagram

There are various methods that can be used to determine the most important risks in a qualitative manner. The two most commonly used methods are explained here, as well as a combination of both:

1. Assigning points to the most significant risks.
2. Assessing probability and consequence separately using numbers.
3. A combination of methods 1 and 2.

1. Assigning points to the most significant risks

In this method, those involved in the risk analysis assign a number of points to the risks they consider to be the most significant. These points are the time, money and effort that are available to those involved for controlling the risk.

The number of points that a participant may assign to the risks is determined by the number of risks identified; commonly 20 to 100 points are used. In assigning points, a number of limiting conditions are given (for example, dividing the points among a minimum of 5 and maximum of 20 risks). This is necessary to prevent one person being able to exert a high degree of influence on the total by assigning all of the points to a single risk, or by giving the sceptic the opportunity to assign one point to each of the risks. The points are added up for each risk and the risks are ranked by the number of points assigned to them.

An example is presented in Table 2.4 in which five participants (A, B, C, D and E) have allocated 100 points to 10 different risks.

This produces a list of the most significant risks, as shown in Table 2.5.

This method can be applied easily and quickly and is useful for bringing together a range of opinions. An important advantage is that from a long list of risks the most significant ones can be selected and assessed.

2. Assessing probability and consequence separately using numbers

In this method, the risk is divided into probability and consequence (risk = probability x consequence). Rather than an 'absolute' estimation of the probability and the consequence, the assessment arises through the use of classes.

Not too many classes should be used, so as to avoid difficulties in estimating or in creating a false impression of precision, when the idea is to provide an indication of ranking in order of importance. It is also important to use an even number of classes so that people have to make a choice – there is no 'neutral' midpoint. Practice shows that it is best to use four classes for estimating both probability and consequence.

Table 2.4 Method 1 for determining the importance of risks

Risk	1	2	3	4	5	6	7	8	9	10	
Participants											Points per participant
A	10	5	0	10	0	0	0	25	30	20	100
B	5	10	30	0	0	15	10	0	30	0	100
C	10	25	15	20	0	0	5	0	5	20	100
D	5	20	17	15	33	10	0	0	0	0	100
E	5	18	20	7	20	30	0	0	0	0	100
Total	35	78	82	52	53	55	15	25	65	40	500

Table 2.5 Risks and scores

Risk		Score
1.	Risk 3	82
2.	Risk 2	78
3.	Risk 9	65
4.	Risk 6	55
5.	Risk 5	53
6.	Risk 4	52
7.	Risk 10	45
8.	Risk 1	35
9.	Risk 8	25
10.	Risk 7	15

To make the classes workable, they should be very clearly defined to avoid any confusion. It is best to give a value to the classes, for both probability and consequence. An example of probability classes is shown in Table 2.6.

Consequence classes

The method of division into classes is applied to each possible consequence of the various control aspects.

Time

In this case, delay is examined. The denotation of the classes is linked to the objective and the definition of the risk analysis. When the situation involves a project result that is completed later than planned, then a value is assigned to the classes that differs from the one used where a later completion of a partial result is being examined.

Table 2.6 Probability classes

Class	Corresponding probability	Description
1	0 to 5%	Unlikely
2	5 to 25%	Possible
3	25 to 50%	Likely
4	50 to 100%	Nearly certain

For example, if the total time required for a project is eight years, then a risk with the consequence of one year's delay is very undesirable, while a consequence of one month's delay is undesirable for a project with a completion time of one year. One possible division into classes is shown in Table 2.7.

Table 2.7 Time

Class	Corresponding delay
1	0 to 3 months
2	From 3 to 6 months
3	From 6 months to 1 year
4	More than 1 year

Money

The consequence for the aspect of money is expressed in a unit of currency. Factors involved may include additional costs as well as, for example, disappointing revenues or profits. Again, this is dependent upon the focus of the risk analysis. An example of a categorization of classes for money is shown in Table 2.8.

Table 2.8 Money

Class	Corresponding costs
1	€0 to 0.5 million
2	From €0.5 to 1 million
3	From €1 to 5 million
4	More than €5 million

Quality

When it comes to the aspect of quality, it is a bit more difficult to assign a criterion for expressing the consequence of the risk. In this case, the degree to which a risk is capable of doing harm to the specified quality requirements (for example, life span, capacity, durability) is used as a standard. An example where life span is used as a quality requirement is shown in Table 2.9.

Table 2.9 Quality

Class	Corresponding decrease in life span
1	0 to 1 year
2	1 to 3 years
3	3 to 5 years
4	More than 5 years

Information

This aspect involves examining the degree to which the project is documented. An example is shown in Table 2.10.

Table 2.10 Information

Class	Damage done to required level of documentation
1	Limited documentation
2	Unsatisfactory accuracy or detail in documentation
3	Insufficient amount of accuracy or detail in documentation
4	No documentation at all

Organization

The consequences for the aspect of organization may be expressed in the level of support (see Table 2.11). Other possibilities are the degree to which the project result is accepted or the manner in which the tasks, responsibilities and authorities are arranged for the use, control and maintenance of the project result.

Experience shows that it is primarily the risks that might arise in relation to time (delay) and money (additional costs) that are estimated in this manner.

The division into classes for probability and consequence is project specific and therefore involves customization.

Table 2.11 Organization

Class	Corresponding reduction in support
1	Supported fully
2	Supported for the most part
3	Supported to a limited degree
4	Practically no support

Insight into the importance of the risks may be gained in two ways: by using a table in which the probability is multiplied by the consequence, or by using a matrix in which probability and consequence are plotted against one another.

Multiplying probability and consequence

The risks are placed in order of importance, from high to low, by multiplying the probability and consequence per risk; see the example in Table 2.12.

In doing this, the values may be obtained by: 1) combining the individual estimate for each risk – the opinions of the participants are combined by determining the average of the number of points assigned to a risk by the different participants, and placing the risks in order based on the number of points; 2) looking at the common estimates per risk, which can be arrived at by discussion.

Whichever method of prioritization is chosen, differences in estimates must always be discussed. This will provide an insight into the differences in prioritization and create a common view of the importance of the risks.

Table 2.12 Priorities resulting from multiplying probability by consequence

	Description of risk	Probability X	Consequence =	Risk	Priority
1	More design modifications than planned	4	1	4	no. 3
2	More land needed	3	4	12	no. 1
3	Additional sound-proofing facilities	4	2	8	no. 2
4	Removing unexpected obstacles	2	1	2	no. 4

Probability and consequence matrix

In the matrix in Figure 2.10, the risks (shown by numbers 1 to 4) are classified according to size.

Using this method, it can be determined beforehand which risks are considered unacceptable (shown in the figure by the grey squares), for which some action will need to be taken.

The advantage of using this method is that it becomes clear whether the 'danger' lies in the degree of probability that the risk will occur or in the consequence of it occurring. This information is useful when control measures are being considered.

When using this approach, it is important that each risk is assessed and that the different opinions are combined.

3. A combination of methods 1 and 2

In this case, a selection of the most important risks is first made on the basis of the assignment of points (method 1). Next, the degree of probability and the consequence is estimated for the most important risks, identified by using method 2. The advantages and disadvantages of the different methods are summarized in Table 2.13.

IDENTIFY THE CONTROL MEASURES

Now that the most important risks have been identified, the control measures for the risks must be considered.

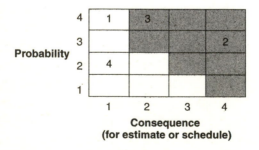

Figure 2.10 Probability and consequence matrix

Table 2.13 Advantages and disadvantages of the different methods

Assigning points	Probability and consequence classes
Advantages	*Advantages*
Quick; it is not necessary to assess all of the risks individually	Forces one to make a distinction between probability and consequence
Provides a good first insight into priority	Less room for implicit inclusion of factors other than probability and consequence
Disadvantages	*Disadvantages*
Room for implicit inclusion of factors other than probability or consequence	Very time-consuming; each risk must be individually assessed

Control measures are defined as measures used to tackle risks, resulting in improved control over the project. The measures are first identified, and then an assessment is made of the effect of each measure.

All sorts of control measures may be created; however, all of them are essentially measures that involve either bearing the risks or transferring them to another party.

The act of studying the risk is often also considered as a control measure in itself. However, assessing risks does not minimize them: it allows further information about the risk to be obtained. This in turn provides insight into the magnitude of the risk or the possible measures that could be taken to limit it. Figure 2.11 shows an overview of the possible measures.

1. Measures that involve bearing the risks

Avoidance

The total risk for the project is avoided. The decision has been made, in advance, not to carry out certain activities or to perform them in a different way. This may be achieved by removing certain preconditions before the risk occurs, for example by re-phasing the plans in the event of 'delay due to frost' so that activities that are badly affected by cold weather are carried out during the summer. Avoidance could also be achieved by choosing another design or method of execution. However, choosing avoidance as a control measure for certain activities could have knock-on effects for other activities, or lead to new risks arising that possibly could be greater than the original risks.

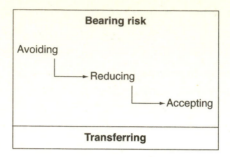

Figure 2.11 An overview of possible measures

Reduction

A distinction should be made here between cause-oriented and effect-oriented measures, given that risk is the product of probability x consequence and exerting influence on one of these factors directly influences the size of the risk.

Cause-oriented measures are those that reduce the probability of a risk occurring. This may be achieved, for example, through the introduction of a countereffect, such as ensuring a good system of communication with neighbours or arranging participation to counter the risk of 'withdrawal of public support'. A cause-oriented measure is established and implemented before the risk can occur and is thus always proactive.

Effect-oriented measures reduce the consequences of a risk. This usually takes the form of limiting the potential damage – by having materials in reserve in the event of damaged materials, for example. Although the probability of damage or breakdowns remains unchanged in this case, the damage has minimal consequences because the reserve materials were available and could be used immediately.

An effect-oriented measure generally involves thinking about the measures beforehand and making any necessary preparations; the measure is only implemented at the time the risk occurs. One example of an effect-oriented measure is having a contingency plan in place, providing an alternative approach should the risk occur.

Examples of cause- and effect-oriented measures

Let's use the risk shown in Figure 2.12 as an example.

Cause-oriented measures are: improving maintenance of the machine; creating clearer guidelines for the use of the machine; and improving the training of the people using the machine

An effect-oriented measure could be: ensuring the availability of a back-up machine so that work can be continued immediately with the replacement machine while the defective machine is being repaired.

Acceptance

The risk is accepted, yet no concrete action has been taken with regard to the risk except that you have become aware of it. As a result, you must increase the margins of the control aspects of time, money, quality, information and organization (for example, setting aside additional money or formulating broader quality standards).

This category of control measures is chosen when the other categories are either not possible or too costly, and if either the probability or the consequence is negligibly small.

2. Measures that involve transferring risks

Transferring risks does not lead directly to the removal of (the causes of) risks, but does lead to a reduction in risk, since it is

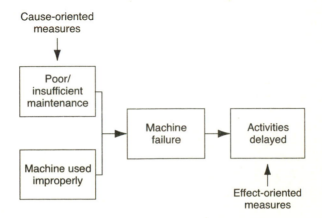

Figure 2.12 Possible measures

expected that another party will be capable of controlling or bearing the risk. Possibilities include:

- transfer to an insurer;
- transfer to a supplier or vendor;
- transfer to a third party.

Any damage that arises as a result of the risk occurring is then compensated for, although other undesirable consequences (deviations in the other control aspects such as delays, for example) obviously remain. Transferring risks often costs money: you pay a fixed amount regardless of whether or not the event or risk occurs.

What is important to realize in the transfer of risk is that risks do not suddenly disappear. Transferring risk involves making agreements and setting out contracts. In addition, while it may sometimes seem sensible to transfer a risk, it may not be possible given your responsibility for the project. If such a risk is transferred, double costs may be incurred: the cost of the transfer and the cost of a claim if the risk arises.

DETERMINE THE OBJECTIVE OF RISK MANAGEMENT

This essential step often appears to be skipped in the initial phases. It is often the case with projects that an employee with responsibility for dealing with risk is appointed first – someone who slowly but surely implements risk management within the organization.

However, experience has taught us that to implement risk management quickly and properly within a project organization, management must first determine the objective of risk management. This is an important precondition for proper implementation: management becomes involved, employees come to realize the importance of their efforts to risk management, and the use of risk management is geared towards the needs of the project organization.

Objectives for the use of risk management in projects include:

- management of the project;
- setting priorities within the organization;
- dividing the risks between the parties;
- basis for plans or estimates.

CASE STUDIES

Management of the project

Risk management is used primarily within projects as an aid in controlling or managing the project. Project management is thus defined as: the achievement of a predetermined goal according to plan. Risk analysis is used in this case to gain insight into the most important risks and to then limit or reduce them through the implementation of control measures. In this way, better control can be gained over the project with respect to the aspects of time, money or quality.

Betuweroute
Within the Betuweroute Management Group, risk management is applied as a control instrument. For the Group, the application of risk management results in the aspects shown in Figure 2.13.

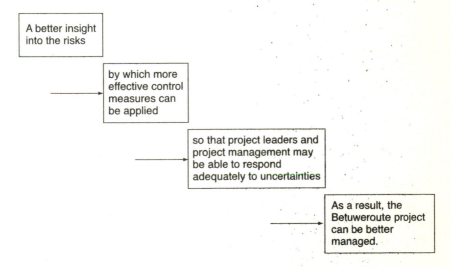

Figure 2.13 Risk management results for the Betuweroute Management Group

Euro 2000

One of the biggest challenges within the Euro 2000 project was the management of the uncertainties and risks that would surface during the course of the project. At the start, the following primary risks were identified:

- inability to conclude the agreements with UEFA and the stadiums on time;
- lower receipts than expected (particularly ticket sales);
- higher costs than expected;
- IT;
- security.

In order to make the risks manageable or to prevent them, or to determine which risks were, by definition, unmanageable, the risks were further examined in a risk analysis performed during the course of the project.

With the aid of a risk analysis, an unambiguous vision was developed for all layers of the project organization concerning the following:

- the definitive and detailed determination of the critical success factors;
- the naming of the uncertainties (risks);
- the categorization of the risks;
- the establishment of the probability of each risk including its probability of resulting in an undesirable event;
- the establishment of the possible consequences and damage per risk;
- the quantification and prioritization of risks (integration of the probability and consequence) and the calculation of the total project risk;
- the focusing of attention on the most important risks.

Subsequently, with the aid of risk management, the following steps were taken:

- naming and quantifying the management measures;
- establishing procedures in the event of risks occurring and taking management measures;
- assigning responsibilities for the management measures.

Setting priorities for the organization

By performing a risk analysis, insight is gained into the most important (ie riskiest) topics involved in the project. This analysis is used to answer questions such as, which topic(s) must receive the most attention? How may scarce resources (people and means) be put to their best possible use?

It is primarily with projects in an early stage (exploratory and beginning study plan) that the setting of priorities proves to be an important objective of risk analysis.

Maaswerken

Those involved in the Maaswerken (Meuse River restoration works) project had a bad experience during the public comment phase: there were more reactions from those affected than expected, and it all took longer than planned.

To improve the progress of the next public comment stage, a risk analysis was performed. During a meeting, various individuals from the project's organization reflected on what was likely to happen, 'simple common sense'. This resulted in a list of possible surprises (risks), for which countermeasures could be devised in advance. Thanks to these preparations, the public comment stage proceeded exceptionally well. Fewer surprises arose than during previous public comments, and if unplanned circumstances arose, these could be responded to adequately. 'By performing the risk analysis, we had the feeling we had already done it all before.'

Dividing the risks between the parties

By dividing the risks between the parties, those involved in projects attempt to gain better control over the risks. One rule which is employed in this process is that the risks must be assigned to those parties who are best capable of exercising influence over them, or those who are best equipped to bear the risk, or those who will experience the greatest advantage or suffer the least disadvantage by 'taking' a particular risk. In spite of this rule, this process results in a different distribution of risk for each project.

HSL-Zuid

HSL-Zuid used this process to draw up a Design and Construct contract for the substructure (all the elements under the rails). The division of risk between the client and the contractor played an important part in arriving at a firm contract.

Figure 2.14 shows the contractor's risk profile as a function of time. This risk profile is shown for a Design and Construct contract as well as a traditional contract.

The figure shows the change from the risk profile between the time of the offer and the allotment during the negotiation phase. These negotiations involved risk reduction and division between the client and the contractor. During this phase, risks are assigned to the party best capable of controlling the risk, and risk reduction is achieved by the client providing an explanation of the potential risks. Figure 2.14 gives no information on the costs (quotation) of the project.

Basis for plans or estimates

Risks may serve as the basis for plans or estimates within a project. As such, the risks are quantified and calculations are performed. The result provides insight into the feasibility of the plans/schedule or estimate.

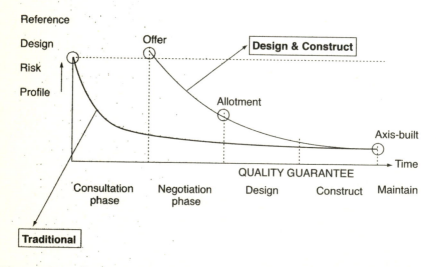

Figure 2.14 Risk profile of the contractor as a function of time

Betuweroute

A quantitative risk analysis was used in the Betuweroute project as a basis for planning. The calculated feasibility of the planning is shown in Figure 2.15 for two risk profiles (RIS1 and RIS2).

In calculating feasibility, the risks are shown as a distribution along the project duration; in other words, in addition to the deterministic duration, an optimistic and a pessimistic duration are also employed. The simulation shown in Figure 2.15 was performed on two networks: the basic network of the planning (RIS1) using the distributions provided by the managers involved; and the same network but this time with the distribution halved and spread among the most important risk-bearing activities (RIS2). This was done to determine the effect of the distribution on the completion date and to gain insight into the most important risks at that stage.

The expected completion date of the project is plotted along the graph's horizontal axis. The probability density function is shown along the vertical axis. The area at the bottom of the graph to the left of a certain value along the horizontal axis (completion date) indicates the probability that the project will be completed before that specific date.

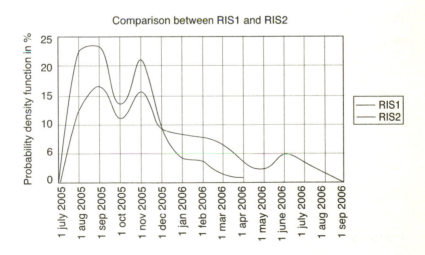

Figure 2.15 Comparison between RIS1 and RIS2

Identify risks

Westerschelde Tunnel

In the Westerschelde Tunnel project, the risks were quantified on a regular basis and their effect on the budget was determined. The results of these types of calculations provide insight into the consequences of the risks for the project.

There are many definitions of a risk. For all intents and purposes, the same definition is used within the projects to describe the concept of a risk. The definition used by Westerschelde Tunnel is: an unforeseen event or circumstance that can result in the failure to achieve the desired result in terms of one or more of the control aspects.

Before starting to identify the risks involved in a project, the goal of the risk analysis is determined and it is decided whether the analysis will focus on the aspect of time, money, quality and/or the other possible aspects such as safety, reputation, etc. In practice, the risk analysis frequently focuses on more than one aspect simultaneously, and nearly always on time and money.

Betuweroute

The risk management model used for the Betuweroute focuses on the potential events and developments that could result in the project suffering direct financial damage and/or encountering delays. The model can be expanded to include events and developments that result in:

- the project (or parts of it) failing to satisfy the technical quality demands placed upon it/them;
- damage to reputation;
- bodily injury.

In identifying the risks, it is often the realistic and sensible ones that are identified. As a result, an initial filtering of the risks is applied to the process.

Euro 2000

The most important risks that were identified at the time (in order of urgency with respect to taking control measures) were:

- More people required to perform activities involved in Euro 2000. There is a chance that more employees will need to be hired than were originally included in the budget so that all the necessary activities can be carried out.

- Options on hotel rooms were taken too late. There is a risk that the prices will rise because options were taken too late for a particular class of hotel.
- Fewer seats in the stadiums than had been estimated. This risk includes the possibility that the estimated number of seats available in the stadiums was wrong. This risk applies to all the stadiums.
- The current press facilities in the stadiums require more modifications than estimated, which means additional costs.
- Antwerp is to be added to the list of stadiums. This addition implies extra costs, which may be charged to Euro 2000 because agreements to cover such an eventuality had not been set down in writing.
- There is a risk that there will be negative publicity surrounding the project.
- Traffic jams caused by supporters. As there are usually traffic jams prior to the start of matches, there is a risk that officials and teams will be delayed by them.

Aids for identifying risks

Aids are often used in identifying risks. In using these aids, a distinction is made in most projects among the various categories of risk.

Maaswerken
Risk themes that were used in the Maaswerken project to identify risks included those involving aspects such as policy, administration, legal, organizational, communication, financial and technical.

The themes served as 'glasses' through which the project was viewed when it came to identifying the risks.

Euro 2000
In the Euro 2000 project, the environment of the project was mapped out to facilitate the identification of risks.

There were many parties directly involved in Euro 2000. The relationships between these parties were complex, mainly as a result of the position and role of UEFA as holder of the legal and commercial rights. Within the project, UEFA acted as client and Euro 2000 as contractor. The relationship between Euro 2000 and UEFA is the axis around which the other involved parties were positioned.

Other parties directly involved were:

- the KBVB (Royal Belgian Football Association) – via the specially established Belfoot 2000 Foundation – and the KNVB (Royal Dutch Football Association);
- EBU and FORTO 2000 (host broadcaster);
- the commercial agency ISL;
- sponsors and suppliers;
- stadiums;
- government bodies (national, regional and local).

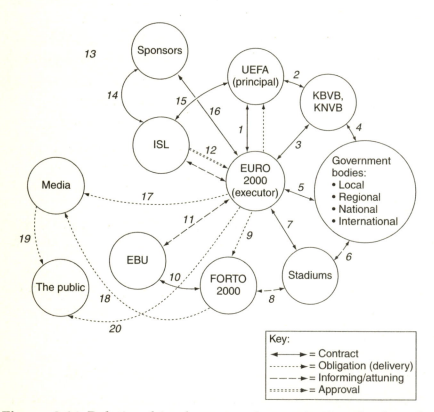

Figure 2.16 Relationships between the parties involved in the Euro 2000 project

Determine the most important risks

Often, a great number of risks are identified for each project. To be able to control these risks, their importance is determined; in other words, the risks are ranked in order of importance (prioritization).

To determine the importance or the size of the risks, the following definition is often used: probability multiplied by consequence, or the product of the probability and consequence of an incident in terms of money or time.

Euro 2000

Risks can be divided into categories:

- standard uncertainties (a risk with a very high probability of occurring and for which the size of the effect is not yet known – inflation, for example);
- specific events (an event with a low probability of occurrence, but the effect of which could be substantial);
- uncertainties in the planning (sometimes it is not known which option will be chosen – for example, which variant will be chosen for the opening ceremony).

All three types of risks apply to the Euro 2000 project.

There are four very important factors involved in risks:

1. The probability that the risk will lead to an undesirable event or effect.
2. The possible effect of or damage caused by an undesirable event.
3. The extent to which the risk may be influenced in advance.
4. The extent to which the risk may be influenced during the event.

These factors have a significant impact on the possible measures that can be taken to reduce the risks or to manage the events should they occur.

Qualitative determination of the most important risks

In performing a qualitative analysis, the probabilities and the consequences of the risks are not described in terms of exact numerical values: rather, textual assessments are used (for example, 'a lot/very little', 'more/less') and/or division into classes of probability and consequence.

In general, the consequences of a risk are expressed in terms of time and/or money. In some projects the consequences are expressed in terms of quality, environmental obstacles and safety.

Betuweroute

The following definitions and classifications were used in the Betuweroute project.

Probability

The probability, expressed as a percentage, of the incident occurring including the related consequences. Due to the lack of statistical material, a qualitative evaluation was used, with the following categories:

1. Zero, in which the reference used is < 1%.
2. Low, in which the reference used is 1% – 25%.
3. Medium, in which the reference used is 25% – 50%.
4. High, in which the reference used is >50%.

Consequences for time

The delay of the entire project expressed in time as a result of an incident. The question of whether or not the direct delay of an event had consequences for the final completion (on the critical path) of the Betuweroute was examined. The categories used were:

1. No delay in final completion.
2. One month delay in final completion.
3. One to three months' delay in final completion.
4. Three to six months' delay in final completion.
5. Over six months' delay in final completion.

Consequences for quality

This relates to the adverse effects on the quality of the final product supplied to the client. It involves an examination of the reliability, availability, maintainability and safety of the railway. The categories used were:

1. No adverse effect on quality.
2. Limited adverse effect on quality.
3. Considerable adverse effect on quality.
4. Very serious adverse effect on quality.

Presentation of prioritization of risks

The most important risks can be presented in a variety of ways. Several methods for showing the prioritization of the results in major projects are described below.

HSL-Zuid

Figure 2.17 was used in the HSL-Zuid project to provide insight into the probability and significant consequences that require extra attention.

Betuweroute

In Table 2.14, all of the possible risk scores (probability x consequence) are shown. Using these risk scores, it is possible to classify risks in order of importance. In the Betuweroute project, this was referred to as 'risk-mapping'. The different risk scores are divided into score classes, each designated by a specific colour indicating the degree of importance. The risks can be classified as shown in the second part of Table 2.14.

Within the Betuweroute project, it was decided that risks with scores higher than 28 had to be considered as 'high' risks. Measures must always be taken for these risks.

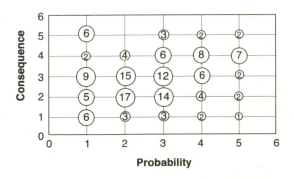

Figure 2.17 Matrix used in the HSL-Zuid project

Table 2.14 All the possible risk scores

Probability												
4	12	16	20	24	28	32	36	40	44	48	52	56
3	9	12	15	18	21	24	27	30	33	36	39	42
2	6	8	10	12	14	16	18	20	22	24	26	28
1	3	4	5	6	7	8	9	10	11	12	13	14
	3	4	5	6	7	8	9	10	11	12	13	14

Total consequence

Low risk	<13
Medium-high risk	13–28
High risk	>28

Euro 2000

With the Euro 2000 project, the most important risks were determined by dividing all of the risks into probability and consequence classes; the results are shown in Figure 2.18. The numbers in the figure correspond to the numbered risks.

HSL-Zuid

Another method used to show the prioritization of risks is by plotting the risk scores against the number of risks. A distinction can be made between the risks for the client and those for the contractor. This method is shown in Figure 2.19.

The client's risks are shown in the dark grey section, and the light grey section indicates the contractor's risks. The lines (solid

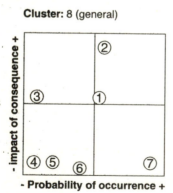

Figure 2.18 Dividing risks into probability and consequence classes

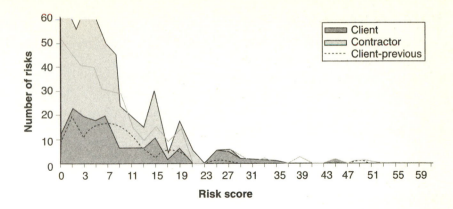

Figure 2.19 Plotting the risk scores against the number of risks

and broken) indicate the risk profile from the previous period. The risk score is determined by multiplying the probability by the consequence.

Quantitative determination of the most important risks

A quantitative analysis is usually performed when a basis for an estimate or planning has to be supplied. It is also used when insight into the feasibility of the estimate or schedule is required.

The probability and the consequence are described precisely through the use of numbers. Using these estimates, calculations can be performed so that, for example, an indication of the feasibility of the schedule and/or the estimate can be obtained.

HSL-Zuid
Figure 2.20 shows the outcomes of a quantitative analysis.

The probability of specific values of the extra costs for the project can be shown using this figure. The size of the contingency items can be derived on the basis of these values.

The advantages of displaying the risks present within the project (risk profile) in graphic form are:

● a picture is worth a thousand words: an overview of the risk profile of a project can be gained in a single glance;
● the figure serves as an aid in determining the most effective method of controlling a risk;

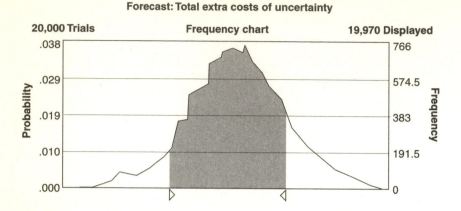

Figure 2.20 The outcomes of a quantitative analysis

- by showing the risks for the client as well as those for the contractor in a graph, it is possible to determine whether both parties are managing their project well (it also shows the distribution of the risks).

Identify control measures

After the importance of the risks has been determined, a decision must be made as to what will be done about these risks.

First, it must be decided which risks will be controlled. This depends on what is still considered acceptable within a project. Figure 2.21 can be used as a tool to do this. In this figure, the size of the risks is shown (classified into probabilities and consequences). The grey portion of the figure indicates which risks are acceptable; control measures must be implemented to control the other risks.

Betuweroute

Within the Betuweroute project, standards have been established for cost overruns, delays, accidents and quality.

These standards provide an indication of what the project organization sees as unacceptable, unfavourable or acceptable. Setting the standards is an iterative process according to the principle of the most feasible. Based on the weighing of the analysed risks, the following steps will be taken:

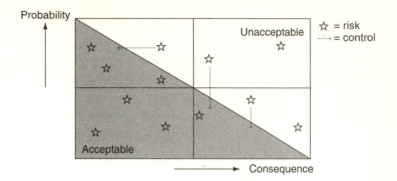

Figure 2.21 Dividing risks into acceptable and unacceptable

Assessment	Consequence
Unacceptable	Initiate immediate, corrective action
Unfavourable	Apply risk reduction measures
Acceptable	Manage continuous improvement

Next, possible control measures must be examined and choices made:

- Elimination. The elimination of a risk entails the avoidance or removal of the entire risk. It is also possible for complete control to be maintained over the risk so that no remnants of the risk remain.
- Reduction of the risk. The probability of occurrence or the consequence is reduced as far as possible, leading to partial control over the risk.
- Transfer to another party. A risk may be transferred to another party, for example, an insurer. Risk transfer entails an examination of which party is best capable of bearing the risk. The best party will (nearly always) charge the lowest costs for accepting the risk. Fees or costs are always associated with the transfer of risk.
- Acceptance. There are risks that are too small or for which there are no suitable control measures available. This type of risk is therefore often accepted and/or monitored so that, if necessary, measures can be taken in the future (temporary acceptance).

Westerschelde
In some cases, further analysis of the causes of a risk is useful in identifying effective measures based on this analysis.

A mind map is a tool that can be used to provide insight into risks and their corresponding causes and to find appropriate measures to control these risks. The advantage of this tool is that it produces information in a relatively quick and simple manner. The tool's graphic display also helps to simplify communication.

The risk is investigated from various points of view (technical, legal, etc). The causes of the risk are identified for each point of view and, as a result, an organization can easily create control measures designed to reduce the risk. The principle of a mind map is shown in Figure 2.22 (the original mind map used in the Westerschelde Tunnel project is not shown here for reasons of confidentiality).

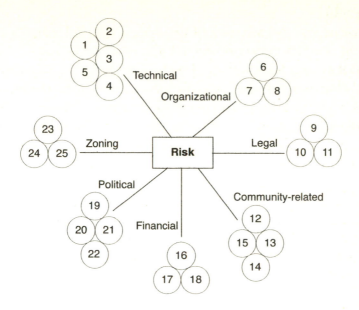

Key

1. Modification in PvE
2. Internal agreements
3. Lack of agreements
4. Project demarcation
5. Project demands
6. Necessary innovation
7. Modification in assumptions
8. Estimation of quantities
9. Possible claims
10. Consequences of errors
11. Insight into procedures
12. Communication
13. Measures to limit damage
14. Strikes
15. Action taken by involved parties
16. Bankruptcy
17. Rate changes
18. Availablity of financing
19. Compulsory purchases
20. Elections
21. Insight into municipal requirements
22. Approval of plans
23. Archaeological findings
24. Soil quality
25. Presence of cables and pipes

Figure 2.22 Risk mind map

3

Performing a risk analysis

The previous chapter described the steps involved in a risk analysis and what each step entails. The manner in which the different steps can be carried out (the actual substance of the activities) as well as the control of the risk analysis are discussed in this chapter.

Performing a risk analysis must be customized to each project and is dependent upon all sorts of factors, such as:

- the phase of the project;
- the size of the project;
- the complexity of the project;
- the people who are working on the project;
- the size of the project organization;
- the objective of the risk analysis;
- the time, capacity and budget available for performing the analysis;
- the quality and degree of documentation required and the intended basis;
- the results required, etc.

For this reason, thought must be given to the manner in which the analysis will be performed for each project. Questions such as the level of detail required, whether a meeting or interviews will be held, need to be resolved during this process.

The first step is to establish the objective and desired result of the risk analysis. Next, the requirements with regard to time, money,

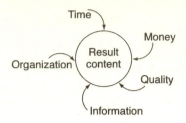

Figure 3.1 The control aspects feed into the result
Source: Wijnen, Renes and Stoom 2000

quality, information and organization are decided and then the actual activities involved in the risk analysis are plotted out.

OBJECTIVE AND DESIRED RESULT OF THE RISK ANALYSIS

The objective and the desired result are determined in consultation with the person or company that has commissioned the risk analysis. The questions included in Chapter 2 ('Establishing the objective of the risk analysis') must be answered at this point.

THE DESIGN OF THE RISK ANALYSIS

A number of questions must be answered for the purposes of designing and later maintaining control over the risk analysis. These are shown in Figure 3.2 for each control aspect.

Time

Agreement must be reached with the client with regard to when the risk analysis must be completed. Should the results be available on a certain date or is there a degree of flexibility? It is also necessary to establish who will carry out the risk analysis. Are there capable people with sufficient time available, are there people who can be made available, or is it necessary to hire people?

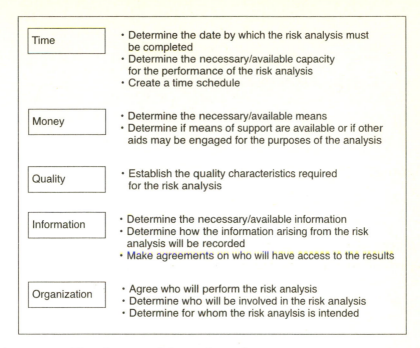

Time	• Determine the date by which the risk analysis must be completed • Determine the necessary/available capacity for the performance of the risk analysis • Create a time schedule
Money	• Determine the necessary/available means • Determine if means of support are available or if other aids may be engaged for the purposes of the analysis
Quality	• Establish the quality characteristics required for the risk analysis
Information	• Determine the necessary/available information • Determine how the information arising from the risk analysis will be recorded • Make agreements on who will have access to the results
Organization	• Agree who will perform the risk analysis • Determine who will be involved in the risk analysis • Determine for whom the risk anaylsis is intended

Figure 3.2 The design of the risk analysis

Finally, a time schedule and limit must be drawn up for carrying out the risk analysis. The time allowed depends on the nature and magnitude of the project and the nature of the risk analysis, but should not exceed three months. A risk analysis is a snapshot in time within a project: if it takes too long, there is a chance that the risks will change during the course of the analysis.

Money

The budget available for the risk analysis must be determined, as well as what the expenditure included in the budget has to yield. In addition, an estimate of the costs of performing the risk analysis must be prepared.

Quality

The level of detail of the risk analysis plays an important role in the quality required of it. It is useful to carry out an extensive risk analysis at the beginning of each phase. An extensive risk analysis can take a few weeks or several months, depending on the number of interviews and meetings necessary.

For smaller, less complex projects, a summary risk analysis, also called a 'Quickscan' (Stam and Lindenaar, 2000) can be sufficient. Within a short time and with relatively little effort, a global insight into the most important risks involved in a project can be obtained.

A summary analysis can also be performed with a large project to gain a first impression of the risks involved. However, it is important to realize that such an analysis is not only 'quick' but also, as a result, 'dirty'.

Information

Agreement is reached with the person or company that has commissioned the risk analysis on the following:

● Which information is necessary/available?
● How is the information from the risk analysis to be recorded?
● Who will have access to the results?

Useful project information for carrying out the risk analysis would, for example, be the most recent decision document (including the project plan, a communications plan, overview drawings, time schedules and estimates). If an earlier risk analysis is available, it is advisable to use this information for the current one.

Organization

In referring to the organization of a risk analysis, a distinction must be made between those people who will be carrying out the analysis, those who will be involved in it and those for whom it is intended.

Who performs the risk analysis?

Before starting the risk analysis, an analysis team must be put together. This may be a team of people involved in the project, although people from outside of the project could also be involved. The advantage of using people from outside of the project (not necessarily from outside of the organization) is that they are able to be more objective in carrying out the analysis, separate from their role within the project. External people require a bit more time to gain insight into the project and to win the necessary commitment from the project team members.

If those involved in the project perform the risk analysis themselves, it is important that they are able to 'let go' of the project, and a generalist (project manager or support staff) is preferred to a specialist (for example, lawyer or designer).

In general, the risk analyst does not provide any intrinsic input to the analysis. The risk analyst's task is to question and trigger those involved so that they come up with new ideas in identifying the risks of a project. The risk analyst can contribute knowledge to this process, but it is the project team members themselves who must indicate whether certain factors truly represent risks within their project.

Who is involved in the risk analysis?

In order to carry out the risk analysis, input from those centrally involved in the project is required. After all, they are the ones who have insight into the possible risks involved within the project.

Those involved in producing the content of the risk analysis can be divided into two groups: generalists and specialists. Generalists are people such as the project manager, planner and the project supporter – essentially those who have an overview of the project as a whole and thus do not approach it from one specific discipline. Specialists are designers, lawyers, technical experts, etc, who view the project from the standpoint of a specific discipline.

Generalists as well as specialists will be involved throughout the entire analysis. In some cases, it can be advantageous to give some thought to the specific contributions of both types of individuals.

Generalists are usually involved when events such as exploratory interviews are held. To gain an impression of the project, a first glance into the risks and the risky topics, discussions in which the generalists involved in the project are present, will be the most effective. In addition, generalists are particularly adept at estimating the consequences of a risk for the entire project.

Specialists, on the other hand, possess specific areas of expertise, which enables them to gain a good insight into the probability that a certain risk will occur. The expertise of a specialist is quite useful during interviews, when certain topics or risks are explored in greater detail.

Regardless of who is involved in the risk analysis, it is important that these people represent a good match for the project's content. This means that those involved can, as a group, oversee all of the aspects and subjects involved in the project. Actually, as was described earlier, it is important to have all of the angles (legal, technical, financial, etc) represented by those people sitting at the table. It is also crucial to strive for an equilibrium between the various disciplines, to prevent certain topics from becoming over- or underplayed.

Finally, a few words about involving parties external to the project in the risk analysis. It can be advisable to involve one or more external parties who have experience with similar projects, in addition to the employees from the project team. In this case, 'external' means a person from outside of the project, but not necessarily from outside of the organization, so an experienced project leader from the same organization could be involved. The task of these external experts is to break through 'project blindness'. It seems to be difficult for teams to remain objective and critical when examining something in which they have already been immersed for quite some time. When choosing external parties, care must be taken to ensure that these individuals do not have conflicting interests within the project that could exert a negative influence on the project.

For whom is the risk analysis intended?

In carrying out the risk analysis, it is important to know from whose perspective the risk analysis is being created and who will or must use the results. The interested parties are:

- the client;
- the project leader;
- the financial backer;
- politicians;
- the project organization.

ACTIVITIES INVOLVED IN THE RISK ANALYSIS

After deciding the design of the risk analysis and the variations that can be introduced, the question is: how do you perform the actual risk analysis?

It may seem complicated, but for a project that is not too complex, it is possible to perform a risk analysis fairly quickly during a meeting lasting anywhere from a half to a full day. Figure 3.3 illustrates the various options for performing a risk analysis.

Essentially, those performing a risk analysis have a choice of using interviews, holding a meeting, or employing a combination of both. However, before this is done, it is sensible to go through the most important information on the project.

The information on the project can also be used to draw up a list of particular points of interest to be used during the exploratory interviews. This list will include the project characteristics, relevant

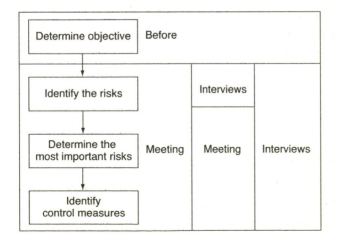

Figure 3.3 Options for performing a risk analysis

milestones, products or interested parties, and can be used as a focal point during interviews or meetings, or as a trigger for ideas. In addition, the project information can be used to create an initial list of the risks or the potentially risky areas.

Ideally, risk checklists should not be used at the start of an analysis. There is a danger that creativity and contributions will be limited. Risk checklists can, however, prove useful as a final check, a sort of verification, to ensure that none of the risks has been neglected or forgotten in the analysis.

Meeting

A meeting is often used to carry out a risk analysis or part of it. The advantage of identifying the risks during a meeting is that a great deal can be discovered in a short period of time. Additionally, interaction and communication take place between the participants and, as a result, a greater understanding of each other's fields is achieved. Often, what one person calls a risk is not considered to be a risk at all by another. By explaining to each other why something is or is not seen as a risk, opinions can be changed.

Experience has shown that an extremely important additional effect of a risk meeting is that by discussing risks, essential information regarding the project is exchanged.

The disadvantage in holding a meeting is that, due to a lack of sufficient interest in such an event, there may be a lack of depth in terms of content. Apart from that, meetings can prevent everyone from making an adequate contribution, which results in certain issues not getting enough exposure.

Prior to the meeting, the following must be agreed upon:

- Who will lead the meeting.
- Who will participate in the meeting.
- Whether or not 'homework' will be sent out before the meeting.
- How information will be processed during the meeting.

It is advisable to allow this type of meeting to be led by one person: the facilitator. Together with the risk analysis team, this person prepares for and leads the meeting. The facilitator is someone who:

- can quickly learn the ropes within the project;
- is familiar with the project-based approach;
- is preferably a neutral party;
- will be accepted by the rest of the participants;
- is not afraid of confrontation;
- can ask critical questions.

The facilitator's most important tasks are ensuring that the participants work together on a joint risk analysis, keeping the discussion clear and structured, and monitoring the progress of the meeting.

To keep the meetings workable, the number of participants should not be too large. The group (including the facilitator) should not exceed 8 to 10 people.

So that participants can come prepared, they could be sent 'homework' prior to the meeting. This may include not only information on the risk analysis and the meeting but also a preparatory assignment or the results of an initial risk inventory. The advantage of having well-prepared participants is that there will be more time available in the meeting for analysing risks.

Information can be processed by:

- writing on flipcharts;
- writing on large sheets of paper with pre-printed risk tables;
- immediate input of information into a computer (and presentations using a projector).

Inputting information into the computer during the meeting will save a great deal of time when it comes to processing the results.

A computerized conference is another form of meeting that can be used for carrying out a risk analysis. Each participant has a PC, all of which are linked via a network. Some of the communication between the participants is carried out via this network; they can contribute their ideas and opinions with a keyboard instead of orally. The advantages of using computerized conferences are:

- Anonymous and proportional contribution from the participants. This type of meeting allows participants to contribute
their risks openly and equally regardless of their function or
position.
- Easy prioritization of the risks. The system can quickly and
easily calculate which risks are the most important, for
example by assigning points to the risks. This takes much
longer when done manually.
- Rapid availability of the results. This is important because the
participants can put the outcomes to use virtually immediately.

Interviews

Another frequently used way of making lists of risks and control
is conducting interviews.

Interviews are primarily used to obtain a picture of the project
and to identify the risks. In addition, interviews can be held in
order to gain more in-depth knowledge of certain topics or risks
or to create a list of control measures.

It is not advisable to determine the most important risks
through interviews, however, as the responsibility of combining
various assessments of a single risk ultimately lies with the inter-
viewer/analyst.

The advantage of interviews is that an initial picture of the
project and the risks involved is obtained (through exploratory
interviews) and interviews also offer the possibility of delving
deeper into a specific topic. Interviews also create an open and
'safe' atmosphere in which productive conversations about risks
can be held.

There are also disadvantages associated with interviews. If, in
performing a risk analysis, only interviews are conducted and a
meeting is not held, there is no communication or discussion of
the risks between the parties involved in performing the analysis. Conducting interviews is also very time-consuming (some
one to two hours per interview). Finally, the interviewer's interpretation of the interview also plays an important role. This can
be a problem when there are contradictory opinions about the
risks within the project.

Tips for conducting interviews

- Involve two people. Two people hear more than one. Additionally, an (agreed-upon) division of roles between interview leader and the person taking notes can work quite well.
- Start the interview with a clear introduction.
- Provide an indication of the objective of the interview and the length of time required, the role of the interview within the scope of the entire project, information on any follow-up interviews, how the analysis will proceed from there, etc.
- Ask only open questions, not suggestive or closed questions.
- Continue asking questions until the problem or risk has truly become clear. Do not be satisfied with a vague description of a risk, but instead continue asking questions until the core of the problem has become clear. After this, if necessary, check by summarizing whether the risk or problem has been thoroughly understood.

Combination of interviews and meetings

A combination of interviews and meetings is used in the majority of risk analyses.

Interviews are often used to gain an initial picture of the risks, which is then supplemented during a meeting where the risks are prioritized and possible control measures that may be applied to the most important are identified.

TIME FRAME FOR APPLYING A RISK ANALYSIS

The actual content of the risk analysis and risk management appears to differ depending on the phase of the project and on the phase being targeted.

The phase of the project

In general, projects all contain exploratory, study-plan and realization phases. Each phase has its own specific characteristics, including the degree to which the scope of the project is fixed and the planning is known.

Because projects undergo development over the course of their duration, it is obvious that the risk analysis and risk management must be adjusted accordingly to this development, and thus change over time.

Depending on the project phase and the project characteristics, the following questions always play a role in the performance of a risk analysis:

- What is the objective of the application of the risk analysis (setting priorities, basis for plans or estimates, distributing the risks among the parties, project management)?
- How should the organization be designed?
- How will information and reports on the risks be provided?
- How often will a risk analysis be performed?
- Is it possible to use risks as a basis for plans or estimates?

Table 3.1 The development of a project over time

Project characteristics	Project phase		
	Observation	Study plan	Realization phase
Result	Result unclear	⟶	Result is clear
	Scope defined to limited degree	⟶	Scope is known
Approach	Globally known	⟶	Planned
Time	Global schedule (in years)	⟶	Schedule exact (in months)
Money	Budget indicative	⟶	Budget fixed
Quality	Unclear	⟶	Quality control system
Information	Not fixed, subject to change	⟶	Information plan Communication plan
Organization	Improvization	⟶	Content determines decision
	Growth and blossoming	⟶	Systematic
	Flat	⟶	Structured
	Flexible	⟶	Clear-cut

Table 3.1 shows the development of a project over time based on various project characteristics. The table is not exhaustive but it acknowledges the fact that the project's characteristics change throughout the different project phases.

When a risk analysis is applied in an early phase of the project, the identified risks often appear to be more general in nature than they are during a later phase. These risks often have more to do with factors relating to the unknown or to decisions that have not yet been made, than with actual risks. In this phase, a risk analysis targeted on the content of a specific topic appears to help in supporting important decisions made within the project.

During the duration of a project, the identified risks become more concrete and specific and lend themselves better to control.

The phase targeted by the risk analysis and risk management

When risk analysis and risk management target the control of the total project, in the initial phase the focus will be on the risk analysis and the step toward risk management is not taken until a later stage in the project.

This does not mean that risk analyses are no longer carried out in the realization phase. The accent shifts from the performance of (often) one-time risk analysis as a component of risk management.

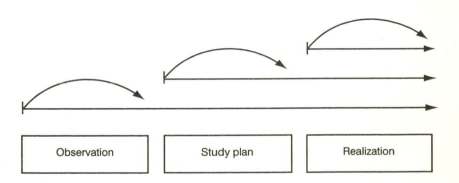

Figure 3.4 Focus of risk analysis and risk management

Additionally, risk analysis and risk management may target the control of a specific phase of a project (for example, the study-plan phase). In this case, a risk analysis will be performed at the start of the phase, and risk management will be executed during the phase itself. The distinction between the focus of a risk analysis and risk management is shown in Figure 3.4.

Activities involved in identifying risks

The techniques used within projects to identify risks vary. The most commonly used are:

- Meetings. This involves the introduction and discussion of risks during meetings. With this technique, a very structured approach is generally not used (such as reviewing the various points of view); instead the risks are introduced on the basis of the experiences of those present.
- Individual discussions. In projects in which separate support has been arranged for risk analysis and risk management, the risks are normally identified through discussions. The supporting party interviews the project employees in order to reveal the potential risks.
- Putting them down on paper (personal expertise). Another way of identifying risks is to have project employees create lists. These lists are discussed again later.
- Special meetings/gatherings. Risks are often identified during meetings held specifically for this purpose. This method is usually employed when external parties lend support to the performance of a risk analysis.

Which of these methods will be applied for each project depends in part on the manner in which risk management has been organized within the project.

Often, several techniques are used in parallel for each project. In larger projects, the decision is often made not to perform a single integral risk analysis for the total project, but instead to perform several analyses (for example, per subproject or contract).

During the process of identifying risks, the realistic and useful risks are often identified immediately, providing an initial filtering.

4

Risk management

The previous chapters have dealt with what a risk analysis is and how it can be performed. Risk management, however, involves more than just carrying out a risk analysis.

The danger comes when those involved think that by performing a risk analysis, the risks have been brought under control. Nothing could be further from the truth – this is just the beginning! Now is the time that the risks must begin to be controlled and when risk management starts.

Risk management is, as was indicated previously, a dynamic process. After all, risks themselves are not static: they can change by virtue of the fact that they are influenced by changes in the project environment, and are reduced as a result of the control measures implemented, even though new risks will tend to arise. Moreover, a risk analysis is a snapshot of the various risks present within the project, with an initial list of the control measures linked to these risks.

To truly manage the risks, there has to be a regular (cyclical) process: the risk management process.

Risk management takes the step towards managing risks through the selection, implementation and evaluation of control measures. By taking effective control measures, the risks involved are reduced. Because the status of the risks within a project changes, it is advisable to update the risk analysis on a regular basis.

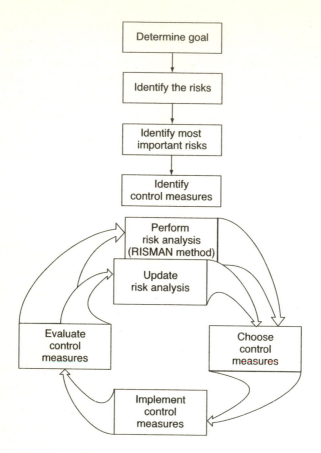

Figure 4.1 Risk management

CHOOSING CONTROL MEASURES

The risk analysis (regardless of the manner chosen to carry it out) always results in an overview of the most important risks and the possible control measures.

After the risks and corresponding possible control measures have been identified, a decision must be made on which measures will actually be implemented.

To make that decision, for each measure the costs, completion time, possibilities for error, uncertainties, reduction in support, expected effects or yields, must be assessed. This can be done in a qualitative as well as a quantitative manner. (See Appendix 2 for a description of the quantitative method.)

If the effect of the control measures is mapped out in a qualitative manner, then an estimate will have to be made of the expected efforts or costs of the measure (large, small, low, high) and the expected effect of the measure (large or small), or by re-estimating the consequence of the risk (lowering it). This depends on the manner in which the risks are prioritized.

Determining which measures are the most suitable also depends on the criteria that are used in choosing control measures:

- Is the measure feasible?
  - Are the means available (for example, financial) sufficient?
  - Are there suitable people available for implementing the measure (capacity, discipline)?
  - Are there other impediments to the implementation of the measure? (Examples of these would be a variety of legal requirements that have to be complied with.)
- Can the risk be influenced, and if so, by whom? In the case of external risks, those that lie outside the area controlled by the project, it is often not possible to implement cause-oriented measures, only effect-oriented ones. It is possible (and often wise) to anticipate external risks, for example, by applying various scenarios and contingency plans.
- Where can the risk best be allocated? Possibilities are parties such as the client ('upstream'), the supplier ('downstream'), an insurance company (external) or the project organization itself (internal). It is only useful to allocate a risk to a party capable of and in a position to exert influence on the risk as well as to bear it.
- Which environmental factors can interfere with the implementation of measures? There frequently is a preference for involving external parties in implementing control measures; for example, will a certain measure be accepted by an environmental group or would it be better to choose another measure instead?
- Does a particular measure bring a new risk along with it or does it increase an existing risk?

Arriving at a choice of control measures is not a simple process. Many different factors play a role. And the choice is made even more complex by the different interests of everyone who is involved in the project.

It is never possible to completely eliminate the risks. It is also not possible to anticipate all of the risks: a residual risk will always remain.

After a choice of measures has been made, responsibility and authority will be allocated. This does not mean that the person appointed must also actually implement the measures: implementation could be delegated to someone else. A budget, duration, and quality and information requirements for the implementation of the measures will also be decided on. The result of this step is:

- an overview of the most important risks involved in the project;
- the measures chosen;
- the people who are responsible for the implementation of the measures;
- the time and budget available for the implementation of the measures;
- the quality and information requirements that will apply to the measures.

IMPLEMENTING CONTROL MEASURES

As soon as the control measures have been chosen for the risks, and a person responsible for implementing the measures has been chosen, they can be implemented. Implementation may vary from taking out an insurance policy, involving the local authority in discussions, transferring one or more risks to a contractor, or using up margins available in the aspects of time, money, quality, information or organization. From this point onwards, a control measure is treated as if it were an integral part of the normal project management.

It can prove useful to first expand on a measure before it is implemented, by translating it into concrete activities and including it in decision documents, progress reports or action lists for the project involved. In this way, risk management becomes a component of the operational project management.

EVALUATING CONTROL MEASURES

The status of the control measures must be examined on a regular basis. Have the measures been implemented or will they be implemented, and do they have the desired effect? Evaluating entails monitoring the measures and determining their effect.

Apart from examining the result of a control measure, it is also important to focus attention on the process that led to the achievement of this result. This can be done by taking a moment to think about points such as:

- What might have led to the desired effect being achieved (or not achieved)?
- Was the frequency with which discussions took place in this regard satisfactory?
- Should the manner in which information is provided be modified?
- Was the necessary information communicated?
- Have responsibilities and authorities been assigned correctly, and why or why not was this the case?

This type of information can contribute to more effective progress of the activities taking place after the RISMAN process.

UPDATING THE RISK ANALYSIS

After evaluation of the control measures, the cycle is complete and the risk analysis will be updated if necessary.

Bringing the risk analysis up to date is sometimes necessary because evaluating the control measures leads to an update of the risks observed. Risks that have either been reduced or eliminated as a result of the measures taken or the simple passage of time can be removed from the list. Other risks might have increased due to changing circumstances or the failure of control measures. Any potential new risks must be inventoried and added to the list. For the remaining risks and any new risks, the control measures to be taken must be identified once again and the cycle must be run through from the start.

During prominent phase transitions within the project, it is sensible to carry out a new risk analysis instead of only updating the current one, because the risk profile can change dramatically during these transitions.

For example, once the routing decision for the construction of a road has been made, all of the risks related to the timely granting of this decision can be deleted from the list. Those risks that are related to further activities, such as completing construction on time, will now be accented even more in the analysis.

Armed with an entirely new set of structured and prioritized risks and their corresponding control measures adapted to the current situation, those involved in a project can now select, implement and evaluate control measures, keep track of the effects of these measures, and update the risk profile.

Risk management is thus:

- controlling risks;
- approaching risks proactively;
- making a list of explicit risks in a structured manner, prioritizing them, devising appropriate control measures and implementing them in a regular cyclical process.

CASE STUDIES

Evaluate control measures

To ensure that neither an excess (too expensive) nor a shortage (too risky) of control measures is taken, it must be established beforehand which control measures are necessary to reduce the risk to an acceptable level. To find out whether the measures taken have had the desired effect, they must be evaluated. After this, they can be adjusted, if necessary, or an additional control measure can be implemented.

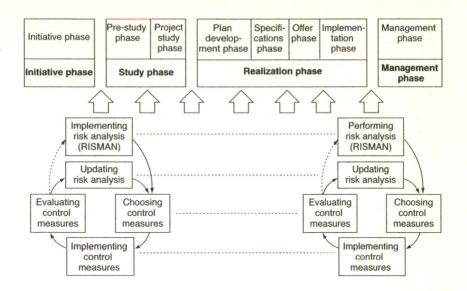

Figure 4.2 Updating the risk analysis

HSL-Zuid

Figure 4.3 demonstrates how the effect of measures is kept track of visually, and on the basis of this it may be determined whether or not supplementary measures are necessary.

In addition to the status of the control measures, the risks are also monitored. Risks change or disappear with the passage of time or as a result of control measures being implemented, and new risks crop up. This situation must be continually re-examined.

The risk analysis is constantly updated. The frequency with which this occurs varies according to the project and phase of the project. In some projects, this process is linked to quarterly reports and the risks are examined each quarter. With a number of projects or subprojects, the frequency is higher; specifically, once a month or once every two weeks.

Betuweroute

Figure 4.4 provides an overview of the manner in which risks are tracked and managed in the Betuweroute project.

A management cycle of risk management is depicted in this figure. The policy and norms for risk management are established within the Betuweroute project. After the risks have been

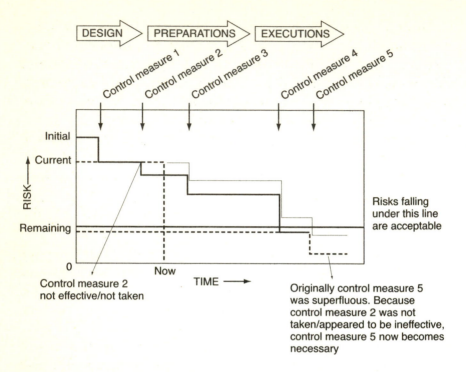

Figure 4.3 How the effect of measures is kept track of visually

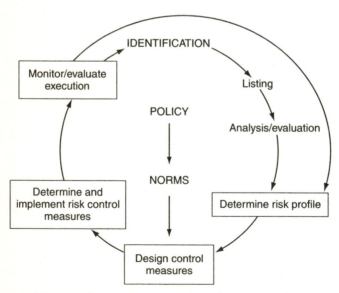

Figure 4.4 How risks were tracked and managed in the Betuweroute project

identified, listed, analysed and evaluated, the risk profile is determined. The risk profile is then tested against the norms. Control measures are only designed for those risks that do not satisfy the norms. After that, decisions are made on whether or not to apply certain control measures. Finally, the control measures are monitored and evaluated.

A difficulty in evaluating risks and control measures is that the effect of control measures is often hard to establish: did the risk not materialize because of the control measure that was implemented, or because the risk simply did not arise?

Observations from personal accounts have shown that the systematic evaluation of control measures occurs too infrequently within projects. This applies to individual measures as well as the risk analysis in its entirety. In addition, it is rare, and only after a risk has occurred, that the question of whether this risk had been previously identified and which measures were taken at the time is examined.

So, evaluation is essential in order to learn whether or not control measures are effective and thus whether or not risk management as a whole is effective.

5

Performing risk management

The previous chapter described the steps involved in risk management. The question now is how one actually implements risk management within a project organization. This chapter discusses this topic in more depth. First, we will describe a number of important starting points.

OBJECTIVE AND DESIRED RESULT OF RISK MANAGEMENT

A number of issues are considered when risk management is implemented within a project, and they are discussed below.

Continually making risks explicit and controlling them

Through the identification and classification of risks, those involved in a project become a topic of discussion. Everyone gains insight into the various risks that the project team leaders 'have in mind' so that the same picture can be disseminated among the project team members concerning the (important) risks involved in the project. As a result, a strong awareness is created within the project organization, which allows conscious choices to be made with respect to the control of the risks.

By introducing risk management into a project, risks will be regulated, at predetermined intervals, inventoried and discussed. In this way the risks will be 'kept alive' and continuous attention will be dedicated to their control.

Dealing with risks proactively instead of reactively

By designating and implementing control measures before risks have actually occurred, it is possible to handle risks proactively, as opposed to waiting until they occur and then taking action to limit their effects.

Dealing with risks on a conscious level and considering the corresponding control measures

By performing a risk analysis, risks and control measures are inventoried in a structured fashion rather than a random one. This results in a more complete picture of the risks involved in a project, and the chance of 'project blindness' is reduced.

THE STRUCTURE OF RISK MANAGEMENT

Time	• Determining the necessary/available capacity for implementing risk management • Deciding at which moments risks and measures will be discussed
Money	• Determining the costs and yields of risk management • Ascertaining whether the costs fit within the available budget
Quality	• Determining the quality characteristics required of risk management • Determining how to guarantee these quality characteristics
Information	• Determining the manner in which risks are to be recorded and reported • Deciding who will receive which information on risks
Organization	• Determining the organization necessary to the implementation of risk management

Figure 5.1 The structure of risk management

Time

How time/capacity can be dedicated to risk management must be decided. In addition, it is advisable to draw up a project plan for risk management. This involves determining the moments or the milestones at which risks and the corresponding control measures are discussed, and reports are created on the risks and the corresponding control measures.

It is important to attune the need for reports within a project to the demand for reports from the organization. These are not necessarily equal. An indicative guideline for the frequency of discussing risks and control measures is once every one or two months. This frequency is primarily determined by the time frame and the dynamics of the project. The shorter the time frame or the more dynamic the project, the higher the frequency will be for reporting activities.

An optimal frequency must be determined for each project. The frequency of reporting on risks and control measures is determined by the existing reporting times within the project.

Money

The costs and yields of risk management must be identified. Possible costs include:

- support from personnel (internal or external);
- (the development of) aids or tools;
- training of employees.

Possible yields include:

- fewer unexpected setbacks;
- less improvization;
- reduced need to look for a person responsible afterwards.

Next, it must be established whether these costs are feasible within the budget available for risk management. The costs and yields of risk management must be controlled throughout the duration of the project.

Quality

The required quality characteristics of risk management are agreed upon beforehand. The quality is determined by:

- what is to be done;
- how it will be done;
- by whom it will be done.

This may be made more concrete through the following criteria:

1. Making risks explicit.
2. Explicit choices for control.
3. Implementing control measures.
4. Updating the risk analysis.
5. Evaluating risks that have occurred.
6. Recording results.
7. Presence of a method/procedure.
8. Monitoring, evaluation and improvement of the risk management process.

Based on these criteria, the (theoretically) most desirable situation with respect to risk management is described below.

1. Making risks explicit

Risk are made explicit by performing the following activities:

- Determining the objective of the risk analysis (the risk analysis focuses on the control of…).
- Identifying the risks.
- Determining the most important risks. This may be done qualitatively (descriptive) as well as quantitatively (estimating probability and consequences).
- Including in the risk description the cause and the consequence.

Risks are viewed from a variety of points of view (financial/economic, political/administrative, technical/implementation-related, organizational, legal/legislative, social/community-related and spatially).

The risk analysis is performed by a 'good cross-section' of those (internal and external) people involved in the project or process, and supplemented if necessary by external experts so that all of the relevant knowledge and expertise will have been included in the risk analysis.

2. Explicit choices for control

For the most significant risks, a choice is made over control (this may be the planning or implementation of a measure, but may also include the 'acceptance' of the risk).

People will be assigned responsibility for the (most significant) risks and corresponding control measures.

3. Implementing control measures

After the control measures have been implemented, they are evaluated.

4. Updating the risk analysis

The risk analysis is updated on a regular basis.

At a minimum, the risk analysis is updated in the event of modifications in scope, phase transitions and/or large changes occurring within the project or process (in other words, if it can be shown that at those times possible changes in the risk profile have been considered).

5. Evaluating risks that have occurred

Significant risks that have occurred are evaluated, and the cause and impact of the risk are determined:

1) The cause of the risk – whether the risk was predicted and whether or not measures had been taken beforehand. 2) The impact of the risk (also on other components or risks) – whether the same or a comparable risk could possibly occur again and whether or not modifications to the existing measures, or supplementary, measures are necessary.

The knowledge gained is stored in a location that is easily accessible so that others within the organization are able to make use of it.

6. Recording results

The following results are recorded and made accessible:

- the results of the risk analysis including the overview of the identified risks;
- the chosen control measures for the most substantial risks;
- the results of risk control.

7. Presence of a method/procedure

A method/procedure for risk analysis and risk management is verifiable, traceable and transferable. The following is described in the method:

- How the risk analysis is to be performed, how and by whom decisions on control measures will be made, how and by whom the implementation of the control measures will be monitored.
- The frequency of updating.
- The various tasks/functions involved in carrying out the risk analysis and risk management and who will perform them.
- How (in which form and to whom) the reporting of risks will take place and when this will be done.
- How much time and financing is necessary/available for the performance of the risk analysis and risk management.

8. Monitoring, evaluation and improvement of the risk management process

The risk management process is monitored and evaluated and on the basis of the results, improvements are made in the process.

INFORMATION

An important element in risk management is the supply of information and reporting on risks.

When money, quality, information and organization are examined, the risks of a project must also be considered. This definitely applies to phase transitions, but it is also important to gain insight into the risks present during the phases themselves. The occasions on which explicit attention is focused on project management, during a monthly progress report for example, are the most suitable for reporting risks.

By properly recording the flow of information on risks, everyone on every level will receive the information they require for guiding that particular portion of the project. This means that the information will be fed in from the bottom up, and that sufficient freedom is given from the top down to enable projects or subprojects to be executed by those responsible for them.

Figure 5.2 shows the manner in which the flow of information on risks progresses.

In this process, each project or subproject gathers information about risks and creates a 'Top X' of the most important. Next, these 'Top X' risks are passed on to the layer 'above' them. Those risks that impact more than just that portion of the project (project-segment transcendent risks) are also 'passed on'.

Reporting on the risks may be linked to the existing reporting structures within a project. Information that may be included in this type of report includes:

- a description of the risk;
- a description of the causes of the risk;

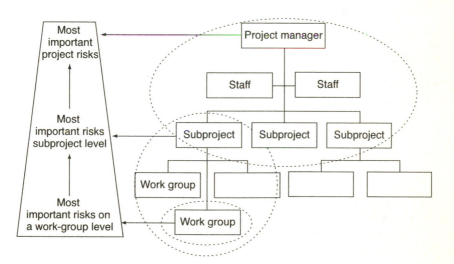

Figure 5.2 The flow of information on risks

- a description of the effects of the risk on time, money, quality, information or organization;
- an estimate of the probability and effect of the risk;
- the potential and chosen control measures;
- the person responsible for the risk;
- the person implementing the control measure;
- if applicable, the progress of the implementation of the control measure.

It is important that something is actually done with the report and that a link is made with successive reports. Why have certain risks disappeared from the previous report? Is this a result of the measures that have been implemented or are the risks still present? When the same risk appears in a subsequent report, has it been reduced, have measures been taken?

Aids

Various aids or tools can be used to keep track of risks and control measures, such as a table (report) or a risk database. The information, in either form, is almost always the same, and consists of:

- a description of the risk;
- cause: description and size;
- effect: description and size;
- (chosen) control measures.

Table

The advantage of displaying the results in a table is that it is easy to set up and maintain. However, when you want to have an overview of all the risks within the project or be able to keep track of them, a table is less suitable.

Another (written) form that can be used to show risks is a report. In addition to an overview of the risks (usually in table form), this report includes the basis for an analysis of the results.

Risk database

Another method that can be used to keep track of and display risks is a risk database. This is an electronic system in which the

Table 5.1 An example of a risk table

Risk	Control measures	Person responsible	Date completed	Status

risks can be shown in an ordered form. The advantages of a database is that all of the risks within the entire project can be entered into it in a simple manner and the information can be retrieved in a variety of ways.

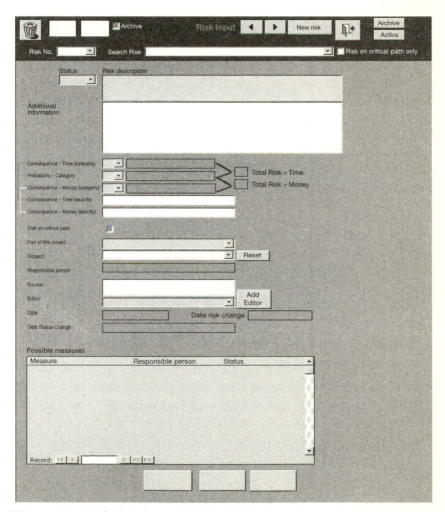

Figure 5.3 Risk database

If, for example, you are only interested in all of the risks that exceed a specific value or in all of the risks that involve the contract, you can select only these variables. Figure 5.3 shows an example of a (partial) input screen for such a database.

Organization

Important basic assumptions in the organization of risk management are as follows.

Risk management must fit in with the existing methods of working

Risk management must correspond to the existing procedures within a project as much as possible. Reporting on risks and the control measures taken will also have to take place on the same level and at the same time as reporting on the corresponding control aspects, for example in the progress reports. Within the consultation structures that already exist within a project, the status of risks and the control measures taken can be reported on by the people responsible.

Risk management corresponds to the level of authority

This means that the responsibility for a risk lies with the person who is responsible for the activities or work that can be influenced by the risk. In other words, each project leader or project team member is responsible for spotting and taking measures for those risks that fall under his or her area of responsibility.

Risk management becomes the responsibility of each project team member

The assumption that the project team members themselves are made responsible for implementing risk management is important to the successful use of risk management within a project organization. It cannot be contracted out in its entirety to an external party, although such a party can perform a supporting function.

Quite simply, everyone within the project is responsible for identifying and implementing measures to control risks within his or her work area. This responsibility cannot be transferred to someone else. The final responsibility always lies with the project manager.

The various roles for implementing risk management are intrinsic, supportive and inspirational.

Intrinsic

Project team members are made responsible for the control of the risks themselves. These are the individuals who bear the responsibility within the project for certain partial results or sub-disciplines. They are responsible for implementing control measures and identifying new risks. This does not, however, mean that they must implement all of the measures themselves to prevent, avoid, or reduce the risks. It is also not the intention that this person is the only one who takes an inventory of the risks.

Certain risks or risk themes will apply to the entire project and so cannot be assigned to one specific sub-result or discipline. Examples of this are those risks involving the organization or the decision-making process. Therefore someone will have to be appointed who is responsible for these risks, someone with the capabilities necessary to identify them and take the appropriate measures. This may be the project manager, but it could be other members of the project team.

The project manager's task is to identify the risks that transcend the partial result or sub-discipline and take the appropriate control measures. Risks that transcend partial results or sub-disciplines are those that can occur within one or more partial results or sub-disciplines, but the effects of which may impact other partial results or sub-disciplines or even the entire project.

Supportive

Due to the large number of risks and the corresponding control measures involved in larger projects, there is a possibility that risk management becomes a difficult process to guide. For this reason, in addition to the intrinsic responsibility for risks, a supportive function is usually set up for the whole project.

Within this context, a distinction can be made between process and administrative support. In the case of process support,

support is provided during the discussion of risks (What is a risk? How do you formulate risks? How are the important risks determined? What are the possible control measures?) and the quality of risk management is preserved.

In addition to process support, it is definitely advisable to create an administrative support system for risk management that involves:

- processing the information available concerning risks and (the status of) the measures;
- supplying information on risks and (the status of) the measures for the creation of regular reports;
- preparing reports on risks and (the status of) the measures.

Motivating

At the same time, someone within the project will have to take on the role of 'risk-booster'.

This booster's task is twofold. First, the 'risk-booster' must stimulate the implementation of risk management and will have to ensure that the people responsible for various activities actually provide the information on risks and measures to the supporter(s) on a regular basis.

Second, this person will have to spread the body of ideas encompassed by risk management and monitor the quality of the manner or method used to take stock of risks and measures and implement them. It is possible for the function of process support and 'risk-booster' to be carried out by one individual.

Risk management can be organized in several different ways. As was indicated previously, it is important to ensure that risk management fits within the existing project organization structure. As mentioned above, everyone within the project is responsible for identifying the risks and taking the measures associated with them. The differences within the risk management organization lie primarily in the manner in which the support is structured. This in turn depends on the size of the project and the project team.

For small projects, the support system already in place can be used for risk management as well. This type of support 'department' includes positions such as a planner, cost estimator and quality control. By 'small' we mean projects in which the entire project team meets at one time and comprises no more than 10 to 15 people.

For larger projects (in which 'layered' consultations take place), it is more difficult to use the existing support structure for risk management as the task can become quite substantial, especially when it involves process as well as administrative support.

As far as the actual placement of the support within a project is concerned, a number of options are possible: decentralized, centralized or a combination of the two.

Decentralized

With this option, the support is incorporated within individual subprojects; see Figure 5.4 for an example.

The advantage of this option is that the tasks designed to support risk management remain relatively limited per supporter, and it is likely that they could simply be added to the supporter's current task list. The disadvantage could be that there is no integral picture of the risks created at the project level.

Centralized

This means that support for risk management is provided from a central level to the subprojects, and that the risks are kept in check on a more centralized level; see Figure 5.5.

This method of organization has the advantage that a good overview of all of the risks is created. A downside can be that the

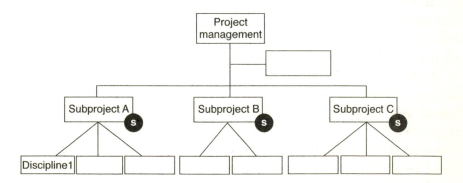

Figure 5.4 Decentralized support

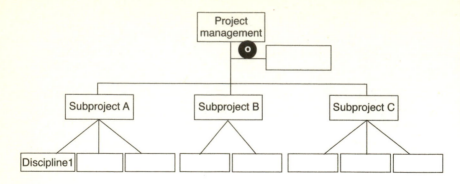

Figure 5.5 Centralized support

supporter's task becomes extremely large. In addition, there is the chance that the risks become less specific for individual subprojects.

Combination of the two

This option involves support on a subproject as well as central level; see Figure 5.6.

This option combines all of the advantages of both of the previous methods. A good overview of the risks exists on all levels. The only disadvantage is that the support for risk management can be relatively difficult.

ACTIVITIES INVOLVED IN RISK MANAGEMENT

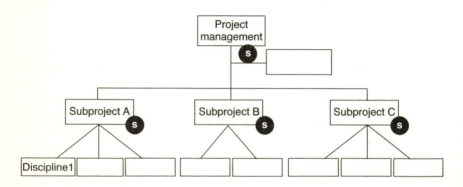

Figure 5.6 A combination of the two

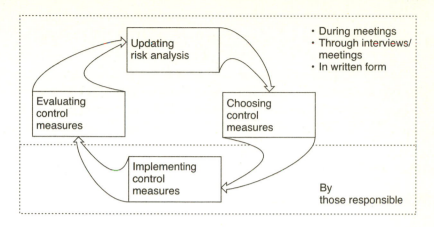

Figure 5.7 Activities involved in risk management

A number of activities must be performed within the context of risk management. There may appear to be rather a lot of them, but many of the steps can be taken at the same time; see Figure 5.7.

The consultation structures already present within the project can be used for activities such as the discussion of risks, the progress being made with control measures, and the identification of new risks. Before this is begun, agreement has to be reached on which risks will be raised for discussion during specific types of consultation events, as well as the frequency with which they occur.

Other possibilities that could be included in these activities are:

- holding interviews with project team members;
- scheduling separate meetings;
- taking written surveys of project team members.

Implementing control measures falls outside the cycle with respect to group discussions and the decision-making process: it is just a matter of putting an idea into practice. As simple as it may seem, experience has taught us that this actual implementation of measures can be a difficult step.

In larger projects, the same types of risk management activities are performed within different levels of the organization. Each step in the risk management cycle can take place on multiple levels. Essential to this process is the exchange of information between the various levels. For example, decisions on major risks and extensive measures that influence the entire project are taken by the project management, but implementing the decisions is carried out by the project team members. This means that communication with regard to risks, measures and progress is crucial. For other types of risks, the gathering of information, decision-making and implementation may be more closely inter-related. Regardless of the situation, these possible differences dictate that attention must be focused on the manner in which risk management is embedded in the organization.

CASE STUDIES

Aids for performing risk management

The aids most commonly used in the performance of risk management within projects are tables and databases.

Betuweroute
An example of a risk table is shown in Table 5.2.
In this table, the possible causes, consequences and control measures are shown for a single risk. The probability and consequences of this risk are also shown by the use of categorization. The consequences are expressed here in terms of the time, money, quality, safety and environment aspects. This results in a total score, which helps to establish the seriousness of the risk.

Maaswerken
In the Maaswerken project, the risk database was set up in the MS Access software program. The input screen from the database is shown in Figure 5.8. The risks and corresponding information are entered into this screen.

When risks are entered, selections can be made from these risks, and these can be examined and printed out in (standard) reports. Everyone involved in the project is able to view the risks in the database from his or her own computer.

Table 5.2 A risk table from the Betuweroute

Means available to management

ID	Circumstance	Possible causes	Possible consequences	Possible measures	Probability	Consequences					Score
						T	M	Q	S	O	E	

Personnel

ID	Circumstance	Possible causes	Possible consequences	Possible measures	Probability	T	M	Q	S	O	E	Score
37	Shortage of personnel (general)	* high degree of turnover * tight labour market * Limited career prospects within MgBr * low level of involvement within MgBr (usually secondment employees) * other major projects (HSL)	* backlog of work * lower quality employees * inefficiency * reduced management of project * occurrence of errors in activities * knowledge loss (historical, project-based, technical and relational) * lack of motivation on the part of remaining personnel	* attention for career guidance and development, for example by implementing an MD programme * Coaching by HRM * Creating combi-positions * Developing knowledge expert system/database * preserve quality through quality control system (preservation of documentation, knowledge transfer, etc) * Knowledge transfer * Setting up structured training programme * Striving for more team-forming	4	4	4	2	3	2	3	44

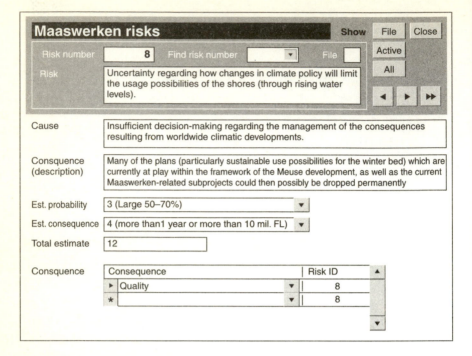

Figure 5.8 An example of a risk table

HSL-Zuid

During the realization of projects, there is a clear division of roles between a client and a contractor. To perform risk management well, it would be best to do this jointly.

A joint risk database was set up within the HSL-Zuid project by both the client and the contractor, which meant that both parties were able to obtain insight into the risks involved.

Both the client and the contractor, in addition to the joint risk file, each kept track of their own risks. This is shown in Figure 5.9.

The maintenance of a joint risk database has the advantage that it contributes to the clarity about risks and to a transparent distribution of risks. In addition, it is possible to make use of mutual expertise.

It is important to realize, however, that not all of the risks are included in the joint risk file as there are always others present that only apply to either the client or to the contractor.

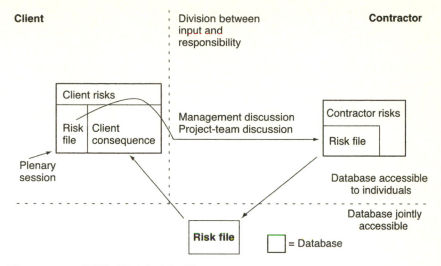

Figure 5.9 HSL-Zuid risk file

Tip. Include the activities involved in a (joint) risk file in the contract with the contractor. The contractor must then take these into account from the start. It is frequently difficult to obtain a risk file from the contractor once the project has begun.

Organization of risk management

The case study companies have organized risk management in a variety of ways. There is no best way of doing this. A project organization must make choices in order to gear the organizational structure of risk management to the particular project involved (depending on the project phase and objective). Questions that play a role in this process include: will a separate risk employee be assigned and what will his or her position be within the organization? Will the risk employee be placed centrally or locally within the organization?

In practice, there are two different forms that are used for the organization of risk management; these are explained below. The first involves risk management with support provided by staff, and the second is risk management incorporated into line management.

Risk management with support provided by staff (centralized)

This form is employed in the Maaswerken, Westerschelde Tunnel and Betuweroute projects. The use of this form involves risk management facilitated by a risk employee (or risk employees). The risk employee provides support in the process of identifying and keeping track of the risks and control measures. He or she also ensures that the risk management tools remain up to date, that the project organization remains alert to risk management activities, and supplies information and expertise on risk analysis and risk management. This method of organization is shown in Figure 5.10

Risk management organized in this manner provides the advantage that the quality of risk management remains secured by a specialist. This person is also capable of accelerating the implementation of risk management. The risk employee can relieve the project employees of certain tasks without having to assume responsibility for the risks.

Here is a quote from the Betuweroute project:

> Risk management does not involve the simple creation and quarterly submission of a list of the possible threats. Risk management is intended to learn the risks and to minimize their probability of occurrence or their consequences in the most optimum manner possible. In order to accom-

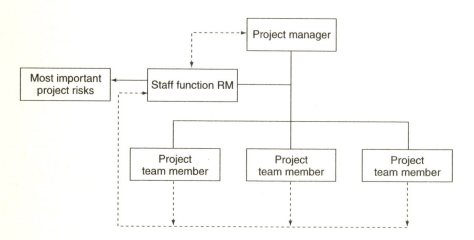

Figure 5.10 Method of organization

plish this, an effective system of communication must be in place regarding the risks and the measures to be taken. The quarterly cycle is a good instrument for achieving this.

The chance does however exist with this organizational form that risk management never really penetrates into the minds of the project employees. 'Risk thinking' is then substituted by the submission of a risk list to the risk employee. There is also a danger that the risk employee will be held responsible for the risks and their control, when this responsibility should always lie with the project employees.

Risk management incorporated within the line of management (decentralized)

The performance of risk management can also be fully incorporated within the line management of the project organization.

It would appear from reports that this is the most desirable way of organizing risk management within the project. However, in practice, support provided by the staff to risk management (initially) still appears to be necessary in many cases.

Within this organizational form, the project managers and the (sub) project leaders are responsible for the practical execution of risk management. These people must be the ones to implement risk management within their project. This is illustrated in Figure 5.11.

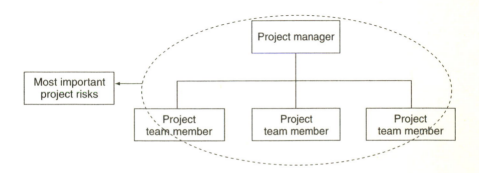

Figure 5.11 Responsibilities in decentralized risk management

The advantage of using this method of organization is that the process of thinking about risks becomes firmly embedded within the organization. Second, the risks and their corresponding control measures provide direct information to guide the people responsible.

What this does however mean is that within the project organization there must be sufficient knowledge and expertise on risk analysis and risk management. In addition, someone within the organization will have to continue stimulating and renewing the process involved in implementing risk management.

This method of organization appears to work particularly well with projects in which a good deal of experience with risk analysis and risk management already exists.

HSL-Zuid

In the HSL-Zuid project, risk management is integrated into the line organization. The line is then primarily responsible for risk management. In addition, there are employees within this organization who support the line and are decentralized. The reason for this is that the HSL-Zuid consists of different subprojects operating under separate contracts. This structure requires a bit of 'tailoring'.

HSL-Zuid and the Betuweroute

Within the HSL-Zuid project, differences regarding the approach to risk management have arisen within the subproject organizations. At present, the idea of organizing a limited portion of risk management centrally is being considered. This central organization will have to preserve the uniformity of the risk management being employed within the subprojects.

Developments within the Betuweroute project lie at the other end of the spectrum: within this project, people are considering placing risk employees from the staff closer to the subprojects (subcontracts). The idea here is to be able to increase the level of customization within the support system.

The example above shows that those involved in projects must continue to ask themselves, not only in the early phases but also during the later stages of the project, whether or not risk management is being organized in an optimum manner. Additionally, it appears that the project organizations share their risk management experiences, among other topics, with one another. In this way, it is possible to learn from other's experiences and to select the organizational form that is best for that particular project.

Euro 2000
In order to implement risk analysis as a practical tool within the Euro 2000 project, clear agreements had to be made regarding which people would be performing certain activities in relation to the risks. The positions and roles are discussed below.

Project manager
- Approving interim reports.
- Ensuring the approval of interim reports by the management and board of Euro 2000.
- Formal assignment of the risks to the various department managers.
- Appointment of a risk manager within Euro 2000 to monitor the control of risks. This position is temporary. At the moment the department managers are able to transfer the responsibility for controlling the risks to the subproject leaders; these individuals will be able to assume the position of risk manager.
- The creation of a network plan or arranging to have this done as soon as possible. This network is considered to be an essential tool in controlling risks involving time as well as money.

Department manager
- Formal assignment of risks to subproject leaders. Until a subproject leader has been appointed, the department manager must continue to carry out the activities mentioned below.
- Agreeing with the subproject leader the frequency with which he or she will be updating the risk analysis.
- Monitoring the quality of the subproject plans on the aspect of 'risk'.

Subproject leader

- Going through the actual risks and control measures as they are described in the reports.
- Modifying and/or supplementing the risks and control measures if necessary.
- If desired, adjusting the qualitative urgency description (for example, 'high') and then translating this into a concrete deadline by which control measures have to be taken. This will form part of the subproject descriptions.
- Selecting the possible control measures to be taken.
- Further elaboration of the manner in which the control measures can be properly implemented.
- Incorporating the control measures and the risks into the subproject plans.
- Implementing the control measures.
- Updating the risk analysis periodically.

Monitor/risk manager

- Random monitoring of a number of aspects relating to the control of risks. Some questions are raised in the process:
  - Have the measures been taken?
  - Have these measures had the intended effect?
  - Should other measures be taken?
  - Is the risk analysis still current, or is an update necessary?

Information about risks

In almost every project, the information flow regarding risks has been formalized. Reports are produced on the most significant risks at least once every quarter. This reporting is also set out in the procedures for project management within large projects. To be able to create these quarterly reports, each project gives the process of collecting information on risks its own personal interpretation.

The aim of properly recording the flow of information is that everyone on every level obtains what is relevant to the person who is to provide guidance to that particular project or subproject. This means that the information is disseminated from the bottom up, and that sufficient freedom is given from the top down so that projects or subprojects can be carried out by those responsible for them.

The manner in which the information on risks is exchanged within the project organization depends heavily on the manner in which risk management is organized. Two commonly used methods are explained below.

Information on risks is organized centrally

Within the Maaswerken, Betuweroute and Westerschelde Tunnel projects, the risk employees are the ones who are charged with the task of producing reports on the risks. The risk employees collect information on risks from all of the components that constitute the project organization.

The advantages of this method are that the risks can be easily compared with one another and that an 'integral risk Top X' list can be compiled for the entire project. In addition, this method allows for the establishment of links between risks occurring within the various project segments.

The disadvantage inherent to this method is that not all of the risks are always communicated to the risk employee, although it is this person's task to keep track of all of the risks and to process them. There is also the chance that the risk employee becomes the person who must take on all the problems associated with the risks; this must be prevented from occurring.

Information on risks is decentralized

This is the method employed within the HSL-Zuid project. Each project or subproject collects information on the risks and compiles a 'Top X' list. These lists are then passed on to the level 'above' them. Additionally, those risks that impact areas outside of that particular portion of the project (project-segment transcendent) are also 'passed on'.

The advantage of this method is that information on the risks remains limited to specific persons/project segments. Another advantage is that information is only provided on those risks that are important to that subproject or project. A disadvantage may be that difficulties are encountered in drawing comparisons between 'Top X' lists.

Table 5.3 A portion of the risk table from one of the quarterly reports

Zuid-Holland Region Supervisory Information Report, Q1 2001. Date: 6 Dec 2001

3.6 Risks

								Consequences	Plan	Control measure Action taken	completed by (line mgr.)	S²
Location	Description	Range	Probability	Time	Money	K¹	Action				(mo./yr.)	
Region	RAW systematics are not in proportion to the systematics found in the quality control system. Contractor claims additional charges to work in compliance with quality control system	Contract	>20%	<1 mo.	5–10 mil.	pm					CM/RD	2
Region	Limited personnel capacity at contracting consulting firms, resulting in high rate of turnover in supervisors and reduction in quality control activities	Contract	>20%	3–6 mos.	5–10 mil.	K				1. Demand progress reports from the contractor 2. Call contractor to account about agreements in contract	CM/RD	
Region	The contracts still to be put out to tender, particularly installations, security and overhead wire, are ultimately higher than were estimated as a result of the pushing up of prices caused by limited contractor capacity (people/equipment/materials)	Contract	>20%	1–3 mos.	10–50 mil.	K				1. Problem which transcends project. Introduce on project management level 2. Sharp negotiations and clear presentation of a programme for demands and specifications. Design contract structure such that the most economically favourable quotation possible may be obtained	RD	1
Region	The scope of tunnel technical installations is incomplete; this causes problems in maintaining consistency with permitted civil and rail activities	Region	>20%	1–3 mos.	10–50 mil.	K				1. Consistency or feedback from realized/permitted work 2. Strive for rapid decision-making as regards scope	RD/DRB	2

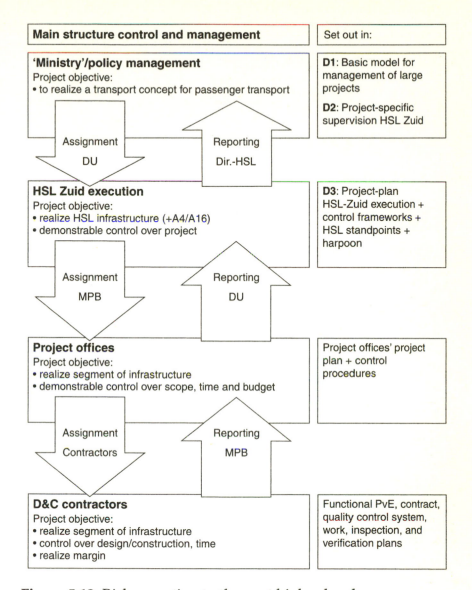

Figure 5.12 Risk reporting to the next higher level

Betuweroute

In the Betuweroute project, the reporting on risks is linked to the existing quarterly reports. Table 5.3 contains a portion of the risk table from one of the quarterly reports.

HSL-Zuid

Within this organization, the contractors, project offices and the central organization are responsible for reporting their most important risks in summary form to the next higher level. This results in only the most important risks being treated within each organizational segment (see Figure 5.12). Each project or subproject acts as the party assigning tasks to the level below it. Everyone is responsible for his or her share and reports on the most important risks to the party assigning tasks.

Which information about the risks should be included?

Another relevant point concerns which information about risks and control measures should be included in the (quarterly) reports.

In designing the reports, it is important that they show the major risks as well as those risks that involve a decision that has to be made on the control measures to be taken.

Betuweroute

Management information destined for the project manager within the Betuweroute Management Group contains:

- an overview of the unacceptable risks across the entire Betuweroute project;
- an overview of the risk action plans relating to these risks;
- the results of risk control.

Management information destined for the risk management steering committee contains:

- an overview of risk analyses, both those that have been carried out and those that are planned;
- an overview of risks classified as unacceptable and unfavourable;
- an overview of risk action plans for these risks;

- an overview of line section overrun risks, the control of which may not be ascribed to a project or process-responsible individual;
- the results of risk control.

The risk action plans contain:

- proposed risk control measures;
- costs/benefits of proposed risk control measures;
- planning of the risk control process.

The frequency of the reports is linked to the existing quarterly reports.

6

Implementing risk management

Unfortunately, implementing risk management within a project organization is no simple task. Project team members are often inclined to view the performance of a risk analysis with a certain degree of scepticism and thus fail to cooperate in these efforts. It is important to recognize this resistance for what it is, and to try to encourage discussion within the project organization. The approach to a risk analysis can help in this situation by finding the causes of the resistance and adequately responding to these causes. Experience has also taught us that those project managers who might have initially expressed scepticism often become enthusiastic, cooperative and participatory risk managers later on. A well-organized implementation, attuned to all of the participants, can play an important contributory role in this process.

IMPLEMENTATION IS A MADE-TO-MEASURE PROCESS

Implementing risk management is a process that must be tailored to each project. One implementation is never identical to another, and each will depend on:

- the size of the project;
- the scale of the project organization;
- the phase in which the project is situated;

- the professionalism of the project-based approach used within the project;
- the knowledge and experience of risk analysis and risk management within the project organization;
- the organizational culture of the project;
- the style of leadership.

RISK MANAGEMENT: A LEARNING CURVE

Implementing risk management within a project organization takes time. Participants need to learn how to think in terms of risks and the application of control measures, which means that people have to adapt their method of working.

Some people assume that risk management can be implemented overnight. The process of implementation, however, has proved to be one of trial and error, and it should not be forgotten that, certainly in the initial phases, the project organization itself must often adjust to this way of working. Implementing of risk management involves a process of 'learning by doing' (Projectbureau RISMAN, 2002).

APPROACH

The implementation of risk management can be approached as if it were a project itself. A number of distinct phases are involved in this process; see Figure 6.1.

Initiative phase

As a logical first step, you must first determine what you hope to achieve with risk management, and when the implementation should be completed. The outcome of the implementation you want to achieve must be agreed upon. It is also important to focus attention on the scope: what will be included in the implementation and what will not?

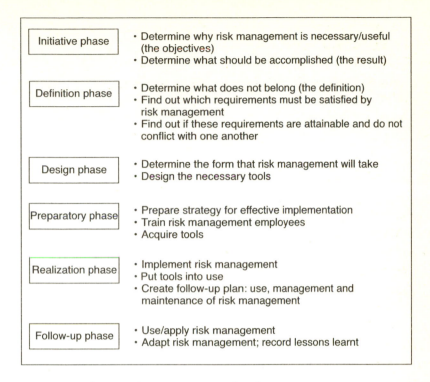

Figure 6.1 The implementation of risk management as a project

Definition phase

The requirements to be satisfied by risk management must also be established. Are there requirements for the level of quality to be attained, the depth to be achieved, the method to be used, etc? Then the requirements have to be examined: are they attainable? Do they contradict one another?

During this phase the need for aids or tools will be examined and the specific functions that these will meet.

Design phase

Next, the form that risk management will take within the project can be designed. This should be in the form of a 'task description'.

Any necessary aids must also be designed during this phase: the shape or form of an aid must be determined.

Preparatory phase

During the preparatory phase, a plan or strategy for effective implementation is made. Risk management employees, if they are considered necessary, are trained during this phase.

Any essential aids for the implementation are also procured and tested at this point.

Realization phase

This is the phase during which risk management is actually implemented; all of the elements that have been devised or considered and any necessary aids will be put to use. The risk management activities will also be staffed at this point.

It is important for this phase to decide on a realistic time frame. Experience has taught us that the time necessary for full implementation (depending on the size of the project) can be six months to a year.

At the end of the implementation, how risk management works within the project must be determined. It is possible that the 'task description' created during the design phase will have to be adjusted, given the experience gained.

A plan needs to be prepared during this phase for the maintenance of risk management. This plan will include descriptions of the use, management and maintenance of risk management.

Follow-up phase

During the follow-up phase, risk management will be used and applied within the project organization, along with the management and maintenance of risk management. This entails regular evaluations, recording the 'lessons learnt' and any necessary adjustments to the method.

Factors for success

The important factors determining the success or failure of risk management are:

- having clear objectives;
- the management style and the organization must be tailored to the specific phase of the project;
- the culture of the project organization must be fully taken into account;
- the position of risk management within the organization;
- the availability of sufficient capacity for implementing and carrying out risk management;
- having sufficient knowledge and experience of risk management;
- external motivation, for example, reports that must be submitted to head office or a parent company;
- incorporating risk management into the existing methods of working and the availability of aids and support.

One of the most important factors for a successful implementation is a positive and stimulating attitude towards risk management on the part of the project manager!

CASE STUDIES

Approach to implementation

Process descriptions of the activities involved in risk management are created in many projects. One advantage of a process description is that the method used to organize risk management can be easily retraced by everyone, both within and outside of the project.

The creation of a process description for risk management always ensures the following:

- the steps involved in risk management are fixed;
- there is clarity on the information that has to be provided;
- the tasks of the persons involved are fixed;
- the risk management system is explicit and 'made to measure';
- the frameworks for risk control provided by the client are tailored to the method and organizational structure within the project, leading to increased insight and support within the project.

In some projects, additional elements are included in the process description such as the terminology that will be employed, the assumptions that lie at the basis of the risk analysis, or the set-up employed for organizing risk management.

In practice, the process description is created once people have gained some degree of experience with risk management. On the basis of this experience, this process description is then further adjusted during the course of the project.

A process description can be a document or be presented in schematic form.

HSL-Zuid

Table 6.1 contains a schematic process description used within the HSL-Zuid project.

The following components are shown:

- from top to bottom: the steps involved in risk control: 1) identify the risks, 2) and 3) determine control measures and 4) update the risks;
- horizontal: when and how information is recorded during meetings and in the risk file;
- the activities that have to be performed for each step in the process;
- in the right text column: which tasks are assigned to the risk manager, project leader, contract manager, project employee, etc.

Westerschelde Tunnel

In the Westerschelde Tunnel project, the risk management activities were linked to the quarterly progress reports. The following elements appear in these reports:

- The process steps: perform or update risk analyses, prioritize the risks, determine those risks that must be controlled, formulate and implement control measures, test the implementation of the control measures and evaluate them.
- The information that must be gathered such as overviews, (partial) results and reports.
- The activities that must be performed including the corresponding roles (actors) and an explanation of the activity.

Table 6.1 A schematic display of a process description used within the HSL-Zuid project

302 RISK CONTROL Revision date: 26–09–01 Existing risk files CL	Projectbureau ZHM	HSL Zuid		
Interviews Plenary sessions Risk file CO	1. Identification	Risk file CL	**1. Risk Manager (RM)** – facilitates identification processes – classifies risks – records items digitally in Risk File Client (CL) **Project employees** – identify new risks – provide information regarding risks	
	2. Determine control measures for CL risks	Risk file CL	**2. Project Leader (PL)** – determines control measures and actions in consultation with RM for subproject risks CL (risk meeting)	
		Risk file CO Control measures/actions for CL risks	– consults with Contractor (CO) on transfer of subproject risks identified by CL which are actually CO risks and transfers them (Project Meeting)	
		Minutes from Project Meeting	**Manager Project Bureau (MPB)/ Contract Manager (CM)**	
		Minutes from Management Meeting	– determines control measures and actions in consultation with RM and PLs for subproject-transcendent client risks (risk meeting) – consults with CO regarding transfer of subproject-transcendent risks identified by CL which are actually CO risks and transfers these (Management Meeting)	

Table 6.1 continued

Input	Activity	Output	Responsibility
Risk file CO	3. Determine control measures for remaining CL risks	Risk file CL Control measures/actions for remaining CL risks	**3. RM** - incorporates Risk File CO into Risk File CL - facilitates quantification of derived remaining risks - determines control measures and actions in consultation with RM for subproject remaining CL risks as a result of CO control measures (risk meeting)
Minutes Project Meeting		Minutes PL Meeting	- together with CO, fine-tunes identified remaining risks and measures - monitors control measures
Minutes Management Meeting		Minutes Management Meeting	**Manager Project Bureau (MPB)/Contract Manager (CM)** - determines control measures and actions in consultation with RM and PLs for subproject-transcendent remaining CL risks (risk meeting) - together with CO, fine-tunes identified remaining risks and measures
Minutes PL Meeting Minutes Management Meeting	4. Update	Risk file CL Risk Top 20 (301)	**4. RM** - facilitates PLs and CM - keeps Risk File CL up-to-date based on the 302A risk report forms from project employees and minutes
		Risk profile CL	- evaluates project risk control by presenting risk profile CL quarterly
Minutes CMM		Completed risk report form 302A	- ensures introduction of Risk Top 20 list during Contract Management Meeting (CMM) in consultation with PLs and CM

- When the activities must be performed. The risk management process is run through every quarter by the NV, and the
  most important risks are reported to the project manager
  once a month.

Within projects, pronouncements are made, indicating issues
that those involved in the project should be aware of during the
implementation of risk management – this is generally done in a
'between the lines' fashion, but sometimes very explicitly.
A learning curve is often mentioned, and the implementation
appears to require customization each time.

Here are some of the things that have been said about implementing risk management:

> Risk management is a growth process.
>
> It doesn't fit in with our company culture.
>
> In the beginning, it was a pioneering process for us.
>
> The leadership style is important.
>
> Personnel are the greatest risk.
>
> Nobody saw the point in doing it.
>
> Management was not involved.

These indicate that in addition to the somewhat 'harder' aspects
such as tasks, responsibilities, information and reporting, the
'softer' aspects such as culture, personnel and management style
also play a role in implementing risk management.

Those involved in projects are aware of these factors, as is shown
by the quotes, but they do not appear to approach the implementation of risk management explicitly as a process of change.

Betuweroute

The process of implementation was taken explicitly into account
within the Betuweroute project. This consisted of the following
components.

Frameworks

Risk management requires uniform identification through the
use of an analysis model, knowledge of risk control techniques
and capacity for the implementation.

Implementation of the step-by-step plan

1. Formalize risk management tasks and responsibilities. Through the use of a formal definition and demarcation of the tasks and responsibilities, the position and function of risk management and that of the Risk Management (RM) department in particular will be made clear to the project organization. This is important for the accessibility of the employees who are directly involved in the risk management process.

2. Establish norms. After a formal establishment of the norms, the RM department will be capable of generating information that is important to the management involved in the implementation of risk management policy (including safety and other aspects) on the basis of the (present and future) risk profiles.

3. Create a plan with respect to risk management activities. A plan for the risk management activities to be performed enables the organization to employ the necessary assets (people and means) in an efficient manner.

4. Agree upon a timeline for the performance of the risk management activities. The timeline is essential for evaluating the results of risk management efforts. The risk management objectives can also be established in terms of time. This also provides the project manager with the means of presenting the risk management policy in concrete terms to external parties.

5. Inform the project organization about the risk management activities to be performed. This involves informing the entire project organization in general about the risk management functions. This provides support to the RM department's function as 'oracle'.

6. Inform those directly involved in the risk management process. Practice shows that it is primarily those responsible for the project and processes who will be the first to be involved and who will be informed of the possibilities risk management can offer them.

7. Implement risk analysis/creation of risk profiles and risk database. The risk profiles form the basis for implementing the risk management policy. At the same time, the set-up of a

risk management database, which includes all of the risk profiles and proposed methods of control, can aid in providing lessons regarding investigating future risks. In doing so, the efficiency of the analysis process is increased: by using various cross-sections taken from the database file, risk profiles for each risk type (category) can be created for each level.

8. Analyse the damage. During the execution of the project, damage will arise. A proper analysis of this damage allows the Betuweroute Management Group to test the effectiveness of the control measures that have been taken (including risk financing) and to adjust them where necessary.

Success factors in the implementation of risk management

To summarize, a close examination of these projects has shown that the most important success factors in implementing risk management are:

- Formulation of a clear objective. Determine beforehand what you hope to achieve through risk analysis and risk management.
- Spreading the message of the necessity of risk management throughout the project management.
- Gearing the management style to each specific project phase.
- Taking the project organization's culture into consideration.
- Determining risk management's position within the organization.
- Having sufficient knowledge and experience of risk management. Risk management must be 'internalized' as much as possible; it must be 'present' within those involved.
- Having an implementation plan.
- External motivation, for example, the requirement to submit a quarterly report to the head office.
- Incorporating risk management into existing work methods.
- Implementation by the proper individuals. The project managers are responsible and the risk managers fulfil a supporting (facilitating) role in this process.
- Making a distinction between primary and secondary activities/issues. The risk analysis must not be too extensive,

otherwise the process of risk management becomes unmanageable. In addition, the risk analysis must provide clear information that in turn provides guidance.

Last but not least, a positive and stimulating attitude to risk management on the part of the project manager appears to be an absolute condition for successful implementation.

7

Conclusion

After reading this extensive description of risk analysis and risk management, you may feel that a great deal of work, not to mention difficult material, is involved in getting started. Once again, we would like to emphasize that risk management is not an entirely new concept, but is in fact one you have actually been dealing with all along. However, what is involved here is making this concept explicit, capable of being discussed, and in which the goal is to minimize as much as possible the risks involved in a project.

Our message is this: ensure that risk analysis and risk management are incorporated into your project and do not make them any more complicated than they need be. The important thing is to get started. Accept the fact that things will not run perfectly or smoothly right from the start. You will learn by doing, and once you have started you will accumulate experience and will ultimately be able to interpret risk management and apply it in a way that is appropriate to your project:

- you've carefully thought out all the angles;
- you've done it a thousand times;
- it comes naturally to you;
- you know what you're doing, it's what you've been trained to do your whole life;
- nothing could possibly go wrong…, right…?

Appendix 1: Checklist for making an inventory of risks

This checklist is divided into the seven points of view mentioned in this book, which are intended as an aid in making an inventory of the possible risks.

LEGAL

- Lack of or insufficient insight into all of the legal requirements and the possible modifications in the areas of:
  - safety;
  - environment (EIS [Environmental Impact Statements] regulations/evaluation of EIS)/planning integration (requirement for compensation of any losses to nature reserves);
  - noise;
  - purchase of real estate and compulsory purchases;
  - invitations to tender;
  - exemptions and permits;
  - procedures concerning zoning plans and regional planning.
- Possibility of claims:
  - claims from a contractor as a result of performance errors that were not covered adequately by contractual documents;

- – claims from the municipality as a result of failure to comply with agreements or damage to the surrounding areas;
- – claims from neighbours as a result of damage to homes or business properties;
- – claims from other interested parties.
- Errors made by the contractor regarding regulatory preparation.
- Errors made by the contractor regarding compliance with regulations.

ORGANIZATIONAL

- Modifications in the POR (programme of requirements) as a result of:
  - – lack of clarity on basic principles;
  - – changes in project definition.
- Lack of project procedures:
  - – modifications procedure, POR, planning, estimates;
  - – completion and acceptance procedures;
  - – AO (administrative organization) procedures;
  - – tender offer plan/procedure;
  - – award procedure.
- Lack of clarity on requirements set by the client, manager, municipality, provinces, etc.
- Failure to enter into agreements with the parties concerned, or failure to do so on time.
- Lack of good communication (internal/external); communication plan.
- Lack of a quality plan.
- Lack of clarity regarding project limits.
- Insufficient or lack of a link between subprojects (internal).
- Failure to take projects in the area partially or fully into account.
- Lack of necessary manpower at a certain point:
  - – problems in setting up and organizing project organization;
  - – withdrawal of key individuals;
  - – modifications in project staffing.
- Late ordering of materials.

- Inaccuracy and incompleteness in the estimate.
- Incompleteness or carelessness in the drawing up of contractual documents.

TECHNICAL

- Incorrect assessment of technologies, construction methods or phases and means.
- Modification in assumptions in design and construction estimates.
- Extra or additional work in connecting new work to existing work in order to obtain good cohesion.
- Applying new (innovative) materials, methods of execution.
- Design modifications during execution.
- Incorrect estimate of quantity of necessary materials.
- Disappointing performance by contractor/designer:
  - non-availability of essential materials;
  - materials delivered too late;
  - construction errors;
  - complexity of execution underestimated by contractor;
  - strikes.

ZONING

- Presence of obstacles or foundation remnants.
- Archaeological finds:
  - possibility of excavations to be performed by archaeological service.
- Presence of cables and pipes:
  - incompleteness of inventory;
  - lack of cooperation from owners of cables and pipes.
- Unusual climatic conditions (long periods of freezing conditions, damage resulting from a storm).
- Additional or heavier pollution or contamination of the location:
  - quality of research;
  - insufficient insight into reconstruction measures.
- Soil quality below expectations:

- soil mechanical instabilities;
- disappointing soil-bearing capacity;
- unexpected occurrence of settling.
- Lack of or insufficient estimate of compensating environmental measures.
- Insufficient consideration of fauna measures.
- Costs relating to ground water protection areas.
- Accessibility of construction location:
    - feeder and transport roads (relationship to other projects, resistance from the surrounding area);
    - insufficient space for construction site.
- Extra construction aids and facilities for traffic and safety implementing facilities or measures for road traffic and shipping.

FINANCIAL

- Price increases for materials higher than expected.
- Rate adjustments.
- Bankruptcy:
    - contractor/supplier;
    - client.
- Availability of financing at a certain point:
    - lack of possibilities for pre-financing;
    - underestimation.
- Non-timely payment of accounts.
- Lack of proper supply of financial information.
- Deviation from assumed depreciation.
- Deviation from assumed taxes.
- Deviation from assumed exchange rates.

SOCIAL

- Lack of good communication with those affected in the local environment, information and participation procedures.
- Extra soundproofing measures to be taken during execution.
- Measures to limit damage.

- Damage as a result of work performed on third-party property.
- Insufficient estimation of facilities or measures required for road traffic and shipping.
- Delays created by blockades/demonstrations by local residents.
- Strikes.

POLITICAL

- Failure to obtain statutory permits and permission or to receive them on time.
- Lack of/insufficient insight into all of the necessary permits.
- Lack of agreement with the municipality/ies, provinces, district water boards, etc.
- Lack of/insufficient insight into the municipal requirements with regard to:
  - method of execution;
  - architectonic design;
  - finishing/repair or adaptation of infrastructure to the environment.
- Problems in adapting regional plans, zoning plans.
- Problems in and with compulsory purchases.

Appendix 2: Quantitative risk analysis

INTRODUCTION

This appendix further examines the method that can be used to perform a quantitative risk analysis, and provides a step-by-step description of the activities that must be performed. As was indicated previously in this book, the decision to carry out a quantitative risk analysis depends on the intended objective of the risk analysis. When the goal involves more or improved insight into the feasibility of the estimate and/or schedule, or when support for contingency items must be provided, a quantitative risk analysis can be performed.

In a quantitative risk analysis, the risks are described in terms of probabilities and consequences. Probabilities are expressed on a scale of 0 to 1, and the consequences in money, if they involve costs, and in weeks if they concern time. These quantitative elements can then be used to perform a calculation in which the following are determined:

- the uncertainty of the total costs or the total duration of the project;
- the contribution of the individual risks to the total uncertainty;
- the consequences measures will have on the total uncertainty.

A quantitative risk analysis as described in this appendix can only be carried out with regard to the control aspects of time (schedule) and money (estimated costs). In order to perform this type of analysis, there needs to be an up-to-date plan or cost estimate. The other control aspects are either difficult or impossible to quantify clearly.

The difference between a qualitative and a quantitative risk analysis is primarily in the manner in which step 3 of the risk analysis ('Establishing the most important risks') is performed.

THE ACTIVITIES

The performance of a quantitative risk analysis consists of three main activities:

1. Quantifying the risks. Risks are quantified as specific events or standard uncertainties. In quantifying the risks, the probabilities of occurrence and the corresponding consequences are expressed by assigning numbers to them. Various methods can be used to do this. Examples include retrieving information from databases, comparable studies ('benchmarking'), using statistics, or obtaining quantitative data based on expert opinions.
2. Calculating the total project risk. On the basis of the quantified risks, the total project risk is calculated for the estimate or schedule.
3. Interpretation of the results. The result of the calculation is a probability density function, also referred to as a risk graph, including the corresponding expected value and distribution of the costs or project duration. The feasibility of the current estimate or schedule can be read from this risk graph. Finally, the most important risks for the project can be determined based on each risk's individual contribution to the total project risk.

The effect of the control aspects can be determined as a final step.

1. Quantifying risks

Types of risks

For the purposes of a quantitative risk analysis, a distinction must be made between specific events and standard uncertainties.

Specific events are those events with a low probability of occurring, yet which have considerable consequences for the project costs, the quality of the project results or the schedule if they do occur.

Standard uncertainties are those uncertainties in the estimated costs or estimated or planned time durations within the schedule that result from normal variation in unit prices, quantities, workable days, and so forth.

NB. Not all of the risks identified in step 2 are included as specific events. It is important to examine each risk and decide if it can best be modelled as a specific event or as a standard uncertainty. In this way, you can prevent double counting of risks or uncertainties.

In determining the most important risks, it is thus not only those risks that have been identified at the time the risks were inventoried in step 2 of the risk analysis which are included, but also the standard uncertainties that have not yet (or not fully) been identified in the estimated costs and/or scheduled activities.

Quantifying specific events

A specific event is modelled with a 'discreet probability distribution' in which the probability and the consequence must be quantified; see Figure A.1.

If statistical information is not available on the probability that specific events will occur, then this probability can be estimated by project employees and/or external experts. This subject will be discussed in further detail later on.

In practice, most people find estimating probabilities difficult. Probability categories can be used as an aid, in which the probability for each category is also expressed in words. An example of a simple classification into categories of probabilities is included in Table A.1.

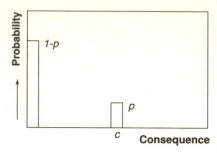

Key: p = the probability that the specific event will occur (probability)
c = the consequence for the costs or project duration if the specific event occurs

Figure A.1 Qualifying specific assets

Table A.1 Probability categories in quantitative risk analysis

Probability category (expressed verbally)	Probability category (expressed numerically)	Probability used in calculation (%)
Nearly certain	p>0.95	95
Likely	0.5<p≤0.95	75
Possible	0.05<p≤0.5	25
Unlikely	p≤0.05	5

There are many alternate classifications. Another possibility is to describe the probability in terms of 'occurs once in every 10 projects', 'occurs once in every project', or 'occurs several times in every project'.

The important point when designing a classification is that someone who looks at the table for the purposes of estimating the probability will always 'be able to imagine it'.

The consequences of specific events are expressed in monetary amounts or in units of time. Table A.2 shows examples of risks for the estimated costs.

Table A.2 Examples of risks for estimated costs

Specific event	Probability (%)	Consequence (x €1000)
More design modifications than planned	5	625
More land needed	5	7500
Additional soundproofing facilities	25	4000
Construction regulations still to be satisfied	25	1400
Removing unexpected obstacles	25	3500

In performing risk analyses, the consequence of a specific event is usually estimated as a single value. It is also possible to model the consequence of a specific event as a probability distribution; this is useful when the consequence is uncertain (see Figure A.2). For that matter, the probability of occurrence can also be modelled as a probability distribution when uncertainty exists. Due to the complex character of this construction (the probability of a probability) however, it is not applied in most cases.

Quantifying standard uncertainties

In general, standard uncertainties are modelled as continuous probability density functions. Usually a triangular distribution is used to do this, which can prove very useful in the event data are scarce. A triangular distribution is characterized by three values: a minimum, most likely, and maximum value; see Figure A.3. However, when the expected value and the standard deviation are known, and a symmetrical distribution is involved, the normal distribution is commonly used.

When triangular distributions are used, a minimum value (if all goes well), most likely value (if all goes as expected), and a maximum value (if nothing is going as expected) must be estimated for each estimated cost or scheduled activity. If estimated costs consist of quantities and prices per quantity, then a minimum, most likely, and maximum value can be estimated for both the quantity and the price.

In estimating the minimum and maximum values of a probability distribution, there tends to a rather awkward element: it appears to be difficult to estimate the absolute minimum and

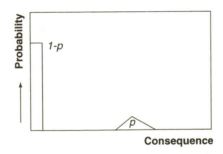

Figure A.2 Consequence as a probability distribution

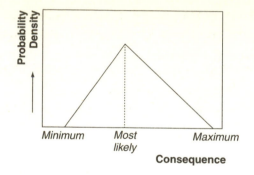

Figure A.3 Triangular distribution

maximum values. For this reason, percentiles are often used when working with these distributions. The following applies here: the x-percentile has a probability of underestimation of x per cent. Although, in theory, all of the possible percentiles can be used, it is usually the 5th and 95th percentiles of a probability distribution that are used. These are the values for which the realization (the actual value) is expected to fall either above or below these values only 1 in 20 times (see Figure A.4).

NB. If it is presumed that the estimated costs in the original estimate are equal to the most likely values, then experts are only asked to provide estimates for the minimum and maximum values (or better yet, the 5th and 95th percentiles), expressed for example as a percentage deviation.

A great deal of attention should be given to the prevention of double counting: specific events that have been quantified must not be included a second time in the standard uncertainties. In

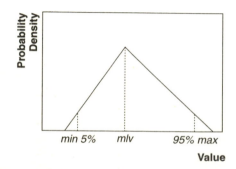

Figure A.4 Using percentiles with a triangular distribution

estimating the standard uncertainties, checks must be carried out each time to determine which uncertainties are being taken into account.

Table A.3 provides an example of quantified standard uncertainties on the estimated costs level.

Points of particular interest in quantifying standard uncertainties are:

● The values that have been included in the existing (deterministic) estimate and plan are not automatically the most likely values. From the combined estimates provided by the participants, it will automatically become apparent where the values from the current plan and estimate are located along the probability distribution.

● In some cases, the lowest, most likely and/or highest values may coincide due to the fact that some of the amounts included in an estimate are fixed in a contract or certain legal provisions apply to the schedule with regard to periods of time (primarily found in city planning procedures, permits and compulsory purchases).

● In a 'skewed' triangle, the most likely value is not the same as the expected value (mean). As was indicated previously, other distribution functions can also be used to model the

Table A.3 Example of quantified standard uncertainties for estimated costs

		Costs (x €1000)		
No.	Estimate item	Minimum	Most likely	Maximum
1	Preliminary design	95	95	100
2	Study	3266	3768	3999
3	Detailed design	5000	5890	7190
4	Purchase of land	21000	22408	23270
5	Re-routing existing road	4500	4861	6790
6	Soil sanitation	9500	11322	12780
7	Groundwork	18900	19225	23700
8	Cables and pipes	3500	3731	4670
9	Construction work	18000	19448	22320
10	Paving	30000	30600	32500
11	Anti-noise measures	7000	8070	9532
12	Lighting	2500	2680	3580
13	Guard rail	5400	5790	6790
14	AA signposting	2900	3189	4465
15	Landscaping	500	575	750

standard uncertainty, such as the standard distribution or the uniform distribution.

In an extensive estimate or schedule, it is often handy to first cluster the estimated costs or activities before estimating the minimum, most likely and maximum values. This prevents the risk analysis from becoming too detailed and thus taking too long to perform. The clustering should, however, not detract from the completeness of the estimate: the estimated costs must obviously remain the same.

Gathering input for the quantitative analysis

The risks are quantified either through using the available statistical information or by asking members of the project team and/or external experts to produce estimates. A group meeting, individual interviews or a written survey can be organized to assist in this quantification process.

Because the estimates produced by experts may differ, it is necessary to combine them to create one assessment. In combining expert opinions, the key is to determine how the estimates will be weighed with respect to one another. For example, a single expert may be chosen, or each expert's opinion may be weighed equally, or varying weights may be assigned to each expert's opinion. One way to determine the weights is through a test. In performing a risk analysis, equal weights are typically assigned to the opinions resulting from interviews with experts, but it is also possible to weigh the experts' estimates on the basis of their responses.

There are a number of methods for combining opinions, expert or otherwise, such as the Delphi method, the classical model, the method of paired comparisons and Bayesian models. For further information, see *Experts in Uncertainty* (Cooke, 1991).

2. Calculating the total project risk

On the basis of the quantified risks, the total project risk can be calculated in the form of a probability density function of the desired parameters. This may involve the total project costs, but can also be the completion time for a project or subproject, if the risk analysis focuses on the control aspect of time. The calculations are performed manually or with software designed to produce Monte Carlo simulations.

If the model is simple and small-scale, the total risk can be calculated manually through the sole use of expected values and standard deviations, but in most cases the project is too large to perform manual calculations. A rough manual calculation can, however, prove useful in verifying the outcomes of a computer-generated calculation. An example of a manual calculation with triangular distributions is shown in *The RISMAN Quickscan* (Stam and Lindenaar, 2000).

In general, software based on Monte Carlo simulations is used. The principle involved is that the project is modelled in a calculation program (using a model for time and/or costs). The model does not calculate the deterministic values; rather it calculates the probability distributions for the individual schedule events and cost items determined in the previous step. A large number of calculations will then have to be run within the modelled project ('simulated' some 10,000 times), in which random draws will be made from all of the probability distributions given. In this way, a probability distribution is created for the final project result.

Modelling

In the modelling of a project, the following issues must be considered:

- degree of clustering of the cost items and/or schedule events;
- modelling of dependencies between risks;
- any link between time and money.

Clustering of cost items and/or schedule events

The degree of detail included in the estimate and/or schedule must be comparable to that found in the risk analysis. An estimate can easily contain several hundred lines, including items whose amounts may range from approximately €100 to €10 million. This means that the costs included in the estimate should usually be clustered. There are various ways of clustering:

- on the basis of objects (eg, tunnel, road, bridge, building);
- on the basis of components/phases (eg, building excavation, foundation, concrete construction);
- on the basis of materials (eg, all concrete, reinforcement, soil, finishing items, steel, wages).

Each project and project phase must be examined to determine whether clustering is necessary and which method is the most appropriate for this purpose.

The modelling of the schedule must be carried out carefully. Simplifying a schedule consisting of several hundred lines is no easy task. Close attention must be paid in particular to the relationships between the various activities. It is often better to combine activities that are performed in series (following one another in succession) rather than those which run parallel to one another. When modelling a planning process, it is essential to keep the critical path intact as well as the possible changes occurring along this path.

Dependencies between risks

Dependencies (correlations) can have an enormous influence on the calculation of the project risk. Poor quality foundations (for example, weak peat soil) can lead to a larger quantity of sand being required, but also the need to construct a more solid structural foundation. It appears that the quantity of heightening materials and the foundation for a flyover are dependent upon one another; in other words, there is a certain degree of correlation between the two.

For a description of the method used to estimate the size of dependencies and the importance of evaluating them, see 'Expected, unexpected or uncertain' (Vrijling *et al*).

In performing risk analyses, the dependencies between risks are often calculated in two different ways for the sake of gaining insight:

1. Complete independence of all of the risks. This method is based on the assumption that not everything has to work out well or badly simultaneously. The result of a calculation made on the basis of this scenario is the lower limit of the distribution around the expected costs.

2. Complete dependence of all of the risks. This is based on the idea that if something should go wrong, the rest will go wrong as well. The result of a calculation made on the basis of this scenario is the upper limit of the distribution around the project costs.

This process results in a picture of the sensitivity of the project result to any existing dependencies. The best possible result is often used as it is particularly difficult to quantify dependencies.

The expected value of the project costs that emerges from both simulations is, however, the same. One must keep in mind that the method described above only determines an upper and lower limit for the distribution and is not a reflection of reality.

Possible connection between the control aspects of money and time (linked estimate and schedule)

Most quantitative risk analyses are performed on the control aspects of money or time. It is only in exceptional cases that the estimated costs are linked to the activities from the planning process and then it is possible to perform calculations on estimates that are linked to plans. This is because of the problems encountered in linking both elements during the pre-project stage. It is in fact difficult to indicate how many additional costs will be incurred, for example, in the event an administrative decision has been made too late.

Schedules and estimates are easier to link to one another for the execution phase of a project. Wages and construction site costs continue to be incurred even if the project overruns its schedule. For this reason, it is important to input those costs that are dependent on time in this type of model. Here's an example.

A project has a total duration of 25 months. Of this, 15 months are dedicated to design and preparation and 10 months to construction. The total project costs amount to €14 million, €2 million of which is assigned to construction site costs. Of these costs, 75 per cent is dependent on time. A critical activity involved in the aspect of time is the concrete work. A period of five months has been planned for this purpose. The costs for this total €2 million, 50 per cent of which is wages.

In this case, a one-month delay in the concrete work activities results in a cost overrun, as shown in Table A.4.

Table A.4 Cost overrun resulting from a one-month delay

Cost item	Consequences	
Building site costs	75% * 2M€/10 months =	150 K€
Wages for concrete work	50% * 2 M€/5months =	200 K€
Total cost overrun		350 K€

Results of the calculation

The result of the calculation is a risk graph (probability density function) with corresponding expected value (mean) and distribution (standard deviation); see Figure A.5.

The costs or the duration of the project are plotted along the horizontal axis of the graph. The probability density function is plotted along the vertical axis. The 'centre of gravity' of the numbers on the graph shows the mean or the expected value of the estimate or the schedule. The distribution is a means of measuring the uncertainty in the project costs or duration; the greater the distribution, the 'flatter' the risk graph will be, and the more uncertain the project costs or duration.

The area at the bottom the graph to the left of a certain value on the horizontal axis (costs or duration) is referred to as the feasibility (or probability of underestimation) of this value. In this way, the feasibility of the duration currently required or costs of the project can also be determined. This may be read more simply if the risk graph is shown in the form of a cumulative probability distribution.

The curve on this graph indicates the probability of underestimation. This probability can be read on the vertical axis for each

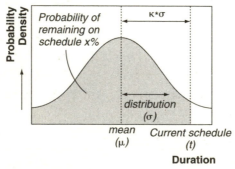

Figure A.5 A risk graph

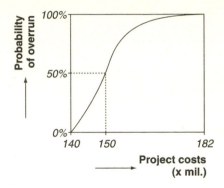

Figure A.6 The risk graph shown as a cumulative probability distribution

value (costs or duration). For a number of striking probabilities of underestimation, the data from the graph (the percentiles) can also be shown, as in Table A.5.

The probability that the project costs exceed €142 million is thus 95 per cent in this example. The probability that the project costs are less than or equal to €170 million is 95 per cent.

3. Interpretation of the results

The results of the risk calculation can be used by the project manager and his or her client as a tool to evaluate the current estimate or schedule, and to adjust it if necessary. The actual decision is made in the step 'Choosing control measures' from the risk management process.

Below is an example of a risk calculation for an estimate that will show how the results of the calculation are interpreted; the results of a risk calculation for a schedule can be interpreted in precisely the same manner. By interpreting the 'basket of risks', a distinction is made between the approach employed by a large client (for example, the Department of Public Works) and the approach used by a supplier (for example, a contractor).

Table A.5 Data from the graph in tabular form

Probability of overrun	1%	5%	50%	95%	99%
Project costs (x €1 mil.)	≤140	≤142	≤150	≤170	≤180

Client's approach

The results shown in Table A.6 were produced from an estimate and the calculation of the project risk.

The 90 per cent confidence interval means that there is a 90 per cent degree of certainty that the final project costs will fall between €142 million and €170 million. The 50 per cent probability of underestimation means that there is a 50 per cent chance that the final project costs will either be more or less than €150 million.

Based on the calculation, the following conclusion can be drawn. The difference between the basic estimate and the expected value of the project costs is €10 million. In principle, the difference between the basic estimate and the expected value should be equal to the contingency items. In this example, the contingency items total €8 million, therefore this is unsatisfactory.

The difference between the basic estimate and the expected value of €10 million (or the contingency items) consists of three components:

- the difference between the basic estimate and the most likely value (€3 million); in general, the same value is used for the basic estimate and the most likely value and the difference between the two thus equals zero;
- the difference between the expected value of the specific events (€4 million);
- a shift as a result of the skewed distributions of the standard uncertainties (€3 million).

Table A.6 Risk calculation – client's approach

Current deterministic estimate	€ millions
Basic estimate	145
Contingency items in the basic estimate	8
Total estimate	153
Results of the risk calculation	
Expected value (mean)	155
Most likely value	148
Expected value of specific events	4
Standard deviation (distribution)	6
90% confidence interval	142–170
50% probability of underestimation (50% percentile of median)	150

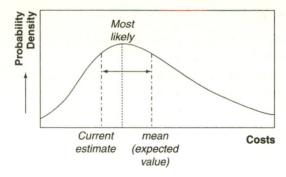

Figure A.7 The difference between the basic estimate and the
expected value

The skewedness of the distribution is the degree to which the
values are non-symmetrical with respect to the mean. With triangular distributions, this occurs when the lowest and highest
values of the estimated items are not symmetrical with respect to
the most likely value.

After the risk profile of a project has been calculated, the question remains, how must this profile be employed? Supposing
that a budget has to be drawn up on the basis of the risk profile,
what is the amount that should be reserved for this purpose?

This choice is nearly entirely dependent on the attitude to risk
of the decision-maker, in this case the financier. Since every
amount shown on the risk graph corresponds to a certain probability of overrun, the probability of exceeding the budget
increases proportionally as the amount that is reserved is

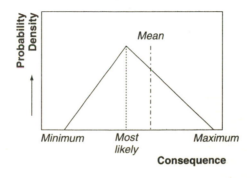

Figure A.8 Skewed distribution

reduced. The probability of overrun can be read directly off the graph of the cumulative probability distribution.

It is thus also up to the decision-maker to determine the degree of risk that this individual is prepared to bear. This will depend on factors such as the order portfolio, the social importance of the project, competitive position, strategic importance of the project, innovative nature, etc. It is important to remember that the willingness to run risks has everything to do with how keen one is to achieve results (those who buy lottery tickets accept the risk that they will lose because they are eager to have a shot at winning the prize). The government will thus have a different attitude toward risk than a supplier or contractor who, given the heavily competitive environment, will have to find the proper balance between profit and risk.

In large projects or a large number of projects, a client is generally driven by the expected value. The underlying idea here is that any windfalls and setbacks occurring within the project will tend to balance each other out on average. It would be inadvisable to assume estimates based on a high probability of underestimation because this gives rise to the danger of encountering underrun. Besides, the expected value is lower than the value that corresponds to a high probability of overrun.

Contractor's approach

A contractor operates under another philosophy in the example described above. For each project, a contractor will need to estimate how much profit can be earned and at what risk. For this reason, the stipulation of a contingency item on the basis of an expected value for costs or duration is not sufficient for a contractor. Conversely, three criteria are used:

- profit criterion: acceptable probability of a desirable profit established beforehand;
- loss criterion: acceptable probability of zero profit;
- exposure criterion: acceptable probability of a major loss established beforehand.

The quantitative substance of these criteria will vary for each project. The indicative criterion is ultimately that criterion which will produce the highest 'profit and risk' increase. An example is shown in Table A.7.

Calculating risk contribution for each risk

To obtain an indication of the most important risks involved in the project, three different types of contribution to the risk can be calculated:

- contribution to the total distribution in costs/duration;
- contribution to the shift: the difference between the current estimate/schedule and the expected value calculated;
- contribution to the feasibility of the estimate/schedule.

If only one schedule is being examined, an additional indication could be the degree to which an activity contributes to the critical path.

The result of this calculation is a table including an indication of the size of the contribution (in percentages) made by all of the standard uncertainties and specific events to the distribution (uncertainty) of the estimate or schedule. An example of a contribution table for each risk's contribution to the total distribution is given in Table A.8.

The 'Top 5' risks with the largest contribution shown in this example are given in Table A.9.

Determining contribution to shift

In this calculation, the relative contribution to the difference between the current estimate/schedule and the expected value that arises from the risk calculation is determined for all of the specific events and standard uncertainties.

Table A.7 Risk calculation – contractor's approach

	Interpretation	Amount	Increase P&R
Basic estimate		€100 million	
Profit criterion	80% probability of 2% profit	€106 million	6%
Loss criterion	10% probability of loss	€105 million	5%
Exposure criterion	1% probability of €3 million loss	€107 million	7%
Indicative			7%

Table A.8 Risk contribution for each risk

Risk	Uncertainty contribution (%)
Standard uncertainties	
Preliminary design	0
Study	2
Detailed design	2
Purchase of land	3
Re-routing existing road	2
Soil sanitation	7
Groundwork	13
Cables and pipes	1
Construction work	11
Paving	1
Anti-noise measures	4
Lighting	1
Guard rail	1
AA signposting	1
Landscaping	0
Specific events	
More design modifications than planned	0
More land needed	16
Additional soundproofing facilities	18
Construction regulations satisfied	2
Removing unexpected obstacles	14
Total	**100**

Table A.9 The 'top five' risks

Risk	Risk contribution (%)
Additional sound-proofing facilities	18
More land needed	16
Removing unexpected obstacles	14
Groundwork	13
Construction works	11

For each standard uncertainty modelled as a triangular distribution, the expected value is calculated with the aid of the formula below. The difference between the expected value of the total costs or duration as a result of this standard uncertainty is determined by subtracting the present value in the estimate or planning from this expected value:

$$\Delta = \mu - x$$

$$\mu = \frac{Min + MLV + Max}{3}$$

Δ = *difference between expected value and present value*
μ = *expected value (mean)*
x = *present value*
Min = minimum value
MLV = most likely value
Max = maximum value

For each specific event, the relative contribution to the difference between the present estimate/schedule and the expected value is calculated with the aid of the following formula:

$$rb = \frac{\mu}{\Delta}$$

$$\mu = p*k$$

rc = relative contribution
μ = expected value (mean) duration/costs
p = probability
c = consequence expressed in duration/costs

The resulting contributions to the increase in the total expected value can be set out in a table in size order.

Determining contribution to the total project risk

So that the effect on the total project risk (expected value, distribution and probability of underestimation) can be determined, a new calculation can be performed using the deterministic value of the standard uncertainty or without the relevant specific event. This is in fact a sensitivity analysis carried out on the results of the risk analysis and is discussed further, below.

QUANTITATIVE EXPRESSION OF THE EFFECTS OF CONTROL MEASURES

As with the quantification of risks and the identification of the most important risks, a distinction is made here between standard uncertainties and specific events. Control measures have already been identified for the specific events. This must now be done for the standard uncertainties.

Standard uncertainties

If a standard uncertainty is involved (a cost estimate item/ scheduled activity with a large distribution), then measures will be chosen that can reduce the highest value of the cost estimate item/scheduled activity. Together with the specialists involved in the project, the causes of the indicated distribution around the cost estimate item/scheduled activity can be studied. These may be attributed to fluctuations in quantities, hours and prices.

Once the cause has been determined, an attempt will be made to identify measures that can reduce the distribution around the relevant cost item/scheduled activity (for example, by concluding forward contracts, or a fixed price building contract, or by conducting research).

The costs of the measure and the effect of the measure on the lowest and highest value of (the distribution around) the cost estimate item is determined for each identified measure for the standard uncertainties. In general, these types of measures lead to a greater shift in the estimate/schedule as well as a reduction in the distribution of the total costs/duration.

Specific events

As was explained previously, attempts can be made to find measures that reduce the probability of occurrence, or measures that reduce the consequences. To do this, the following aspects must be established:

- the costs of the measure;
- the effect of the measure on the probability: the new probability;
- the effect of the measure on the consequence: the new consequence.

Performing calculations

Using the quantified control measures, calculations can be carried out on predictions involving the expected final result of the specific project.

If a standard uncertainty is involved, then the lowest and highest values of (the distribution around) the specific cost estimate item in the original calculation are adjusted and the new values are put in to the estimate. In addition, the costs of the measure (the costs that must be incurred in order to reduce this distribution) are included as an item in the estimate.

For each specific event, an adjusted probability and consequence are input for each measure, and the costs of the measure are included as an additional estimate item in the calculations. This is done in the following way:

- the costs of the measure are input as a cost estimate item;
- the size of the probability and/or the consequence of the specific event are changed or, in some cases, the risk disappears completely (avoiding the risk);
- a new expected value and standard deviation result;
- the new expected value and standard deviation are compared with the previous (initial) expected value and standard deviation and the difference between these values is calculated and recorded by the analysis team (see example).

The result is an overview of the increase or decrease in the original expected value and standard deviation for each measure. This is in fact a sensitivity analysis of the risks. It goes without saying that this analysis concentrates on the largest risks from the prior quantitative analysis (this can also be used for those risks which contribute the most to the shift as well as those risks which contribute the most to the distribution of the result).

Analysing the results

For each measure, the new expected value and standard deviation are compared with the original expected value and standard deviation. A measure's result can be divided into four categories. As a result of a measure:

Table A.10 A table for listing prioritized lists

Risk	Possible measures	Effort/costs	Effect
1.		high/low	large/small
2.			
3.			

1. the expected value of the project costs and the standard deviation may both drop;
2. the expected value of the project costs and the standard deviation may both rise;
3. the expected value of the project costs may rise and the standard deviation may drop;
4. the expected value of the project costs may drop and the standard deviation may rise.

The determination of those measures that are now the most suitable depends on additional criteria that are examined in the selection of control measures. Depending on the objectives and the nature of the largest problems (time or money, shift in the result or uncertainty of the result), a choice can be made from the proposed measures. There are, however, other considerations that may determine whether or not a measure should be applied:

- risk-avoiding or risk-seeking behaviour (evident from criteria such as those used by a contractor, for example);
- 'scoring' several aspects simultaneously (time, money, quality, safety);
- image/reputation risks, for example, with risks involved in an extended out-of-service period;
- the inability to bear a risk financially.

IN CONCLUSION

In performing a quantitative risk analysis, it is important to realize that:

- This type of analysis requires a great deal of time and effort. Those carrying out this type of analysis must consider very carefully beforehand whether the effort is worth the results (expected additional value as a result of the quantitative analysis).
- Quantitative risk analysis is not an exact science. Carrying out the analysis will nearly always involve using the estimates of experts, and the outcome of the analysis should be viewed with this in mind.
- There is a chance that the results of this type of analysis take on a life of their own. It has been known for numerical outcomes to be viewed as 'absolutes', without taking into account the underlying assumptions and starting points.

References

Cooke, R M (1991) *Experts in Uncertainty*

Groote, G, Hugenholtz-Sasse, *et al* (2000) *Projecten Leiden* (Leading Projects)

Projectbureau RISMAN (2002) *Risicomanagement, Praktijkervaringen aan de hand van de grote infrastructuurprojecten in Nederland* (Risk Management, Practical experiences based on major infrastructure projects in the Netherlands)

Stam, D and Blazer, J (1996) *De RISMAN-methode, een instrument voor het risicomanagement van grote infrastructuurprojecten* (The RISMAN method, a tool for risk management within major infrastructure projects)

Stam, D and Lindenaar, F (2000) *De RISMAN Quickscan voor planningen* (The RISMAN Quickscan for Plans)

Stam, D and Verstegen, C J P (1998) *Het RISMAN proces, risicomanagement voor infrastructuurprojecten* (The RISMAN process, risk management for infrastructure projects)

Vrijling, J K *et al* (date) *Cursusmap 'Voorzien, onvoorzien en onzeker'* (Expected, unexpected and uncertain), *Stichting Post Academisch Onderwijs*

Wijnen, G, Renes, W and Storm, P (2000) *Projectmatig werken* (Project-based Approach)

Index